Inside
Apple

Inside Apple

How America's Most Admired—
and Secretive—Company
Really Works

ADAM LASHINSKY

**BUSINESS
PLUS**

NEW YORK   BOSTON

Business Plus
Hachette Book Group
237 Park Avenue
New York, NY 10017

www.HachetteBookGroup.com

Printed in the United States of America

RRD-C

First Edition: January 2012

Business Plus is an imprint of Grand Central Publishing.
The Business Plus name and logo are trademarks of Hachette Book Group, Inc.

The Hachette Speakers Bureau provides a wide range of authors for speaking events. To find out more, go to www.hachettespeakersbureau.com or call (866) 376-6591.

The publisher is not responsible for websites (or their content) that are not owned by the publisher.

10 9 8 7 6 5 4 3

Library of Congress Cataloging-in-Publication Data
Lashinsky, Adam.
    Inside Apple : how America's most admired—and secretive—company really works / by Adam Lashinsky.—1st ed.
      p. cm.
    ISBN 978-1-4555-1215-7
  1. Apple Computer, Inc.   2. Computer industry—United States—Management.   3. Corporate culture—United States.   4. Success in business—United States.   I. Title.

  HD9696.2.U64A6737 2012
  338.7'61004160973—dc23

                        2011044773

For Marcia, Ruth, and Leah

CONTENTS

APPLE'S CORE

An unconventional org chart for an unconventional organization. CEO Tim Cook is at the center, and the reporting structure is just one of many ways that Apple differs from other corporations. This chart, conceptualized by graphic designer David Foster, is based on the author's reporting in addition to some limited information Apple releases publicly.

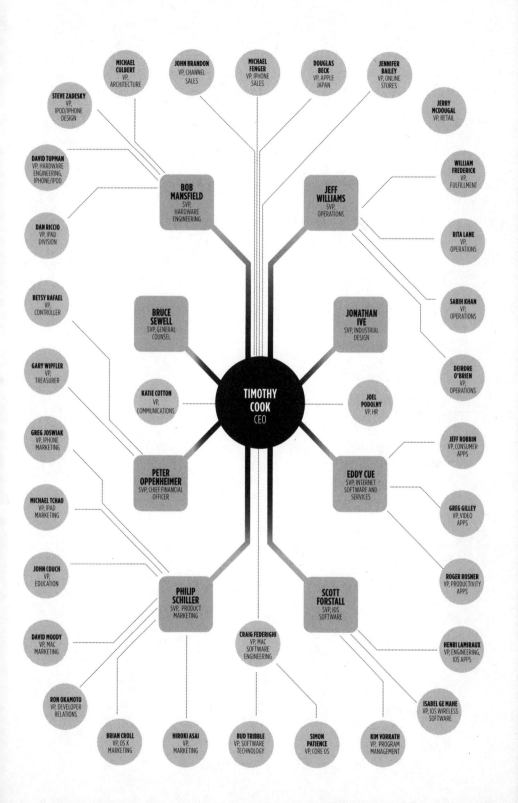

Inside
Apple

1

Rethink Leadership

On August 24, 2011, the day Steve Jobs resigned as chief executive officer of Apple, he attended a meeting of the company's board of directors. He was gravely ill and had reached the conclusion that it was time to relinquish his post. He became chairman of the board that day, giving some hope to Apple's employees, customers, and investors alike that he'd continue to exert influence on the company and be around for a while longer.

What Jobs loved most was products. Though he came that day to tell his directors in person that he was stepping down, he also knew he'd be able to see Apple's latest offerings. Indeed, Apple was weeks away from introducing its newest iPhone, which would for the first time include the artificial intelligence–powered personal assistant software called Siri. Like the HAL computer in Stanley Kubrick's *2001: A Space Odyssey*, Siri answered questions. It talked back to its owner. It began to fulfill

one of the promises of the computer revolution that Steve
Jobs had helped start twenty-five years earlier, to harness
the power of computers to improve human life.

Scott Forstall, Apple's top executive for mobile software, was demonstrating Siri to the board when Jobs
interrupted him. "Let me have the phone," Jobs said, indi-
cating that he wanted to try the personal assistant technology for himself. Forstall, who had worked for Jobs his
entire career, first at NeXT and then at Apple, hesitated.
He was an engineer with the theatrical flair, ambition,
charisma, and raw intelligence of Jobs. Yet Forstall's hesi-
tation was warranted: The whole allure of Siri was that it
learned its master's voice over time by adapting to quirks
and absorbing personal details. The machine was like a
baseball glove molded to its owner's hand, and this particular unit knew Forstall. For all sorts of reasons—Jobs's
notorious short temper, this being an emotional day to
begin with, the stress of handing over an unfinished product so close to its launch date—Forstall was reluctant to
give the phone to Jobs. "Be careful now," he said to a man
who had never been careful in his life. "I have it pretty
much attuned to my voice."

Jobs, typically, wasn't taking no for an answer. "Give
me the phone," he barked, prompting Forstall to walk
around the table and hand over the device. The ailing
Jobs, who had overseen the purchase of the start-up company that invented Siri's technology, tossed the computer
a couple of softballs. Then he turned existential, asking,
"Are you a man or are you a woman?" Responded Siri: "I
have not been assigned a gender, sir." Laughter ensued,
and with it some relief.

Siri's gender-identification issues might have been a

lighthearted moment during a difficult meeting for the board, but when Jobs grabbed the iPhone prototype a jolt of anxiety undoubtedly coursed through Forstall. The scene illustrates many of the principles that make Apple great—but also different from most companies that are held up as models of good management. A giant company had concentrated its best manpower on a single product. The product had been developed in extreme secrecy, and the phone's mechanics and design reflected an obsessive focus on detail. Also on display, for the last time, was a different breed of CEO, one who exhibited personality traits—narcissism, whimsy, disregard for the feelings of others—that society normally dismisses as negatives. But are they? For the way Apple does business and the way its executives manage the company fly in the face of years of business school teaching, begging the question: Is Apple's success unique, or is Apple on to something the rest of the business world ought to be emulating?

It is fitting that Jobs's last official act was reviewing an iPhone, given that Apple's reinvention and domination of the smartphone category four years earlier had demonstrated the company's and Jobs's singular strengths. When it launched the iPhone in 2007, Jobs had turned Apple upside down to make it happen. He envisioned the iPhone as a revolutionary device combining the convenience of a smartphone with the music storage and listening capability of an iPod. If marrying these two inventions wasn't enough of a challenge, there was the additional pressure that the resulting device needed to have a design-snob-worthy look, a user-friendly software interface, and a wow factor (touch-sensitive glass screen, anyone?).

The iPhone team at the time already was stretched

thin. Its very existence was putting strains on the rest of the company. Raids on other Apple groups, Macintosh software development in particular, had ground other projects to a halt; the latest version of the Mac's operating system was delayed because the engineers writing the code had been switched to iPhone work. Resentment simmered among employees who were not chosen for the project because suddenly their electronic ID badges stopped working in areas that had been cordoned off and reserved for iPhone development. All Apple products are created equally; some are more equal than others.

An elite within an elite had been created, and the push to finish the iPhone was like an all-out mobilization for war. Engineers used macabre military terminology at Apple to describe the phase of product development when a launch approaches: the death march.

It is not every CEO who could ask and expect his most talented employees to work through the holidays, as Jobs did for years when the annual Macworld trade show was held shortly after New Year's Day. But Jobs loomed larger than life for Apple employees. He had founded the company in 1976 with his chum Stephen Wozniak. He spearheaded the development of the Mac in the early 1980s, quit in disgust in 1985 when the CEO he'd selected to run the company reduced his authority, and returned triumphantly in 1997 to rescue a beleaguered company. Nearly a decade later, Apple reigned as the brightest light in the constellation of personal-technology companies, and its lodestar unquestionably was Steve Jobs.

Even when he wasn't walking through the hallways of Apple, Jobs was a visible CEO. Sure, his office in the 1 Infinite Loop building was off limits to most of the company. Yet Jobs was supremely present in the life of Apple. Employees of all stripes saw him in the company cafeteria, usually chatting with his design chief and alter ego, Jonathan Ive. They would spot him walking around campus, and they would see his car parked in front of IL-1. They watched his keynote presentations as eagerly as the public did so they could understand where their company was headed. Jobs may well have been unapproachable, and odds were that typical employees would never attend a meeting with him. But they believed that whatever they were working on would be seen, eventually, by "Steve." For all flowed up to him, and his fingerprints were on everything important that Apple did.

On the eve of the original iPhone launch, Jobs was at the peak of his faculties and the top of his game. He had seemingly beaten cancer, having survived the removal of a malignant tumor from his pancreas two years earlier. He had disclosed little about his illness, other than that it wasn't the predominant kind of pancreatic cancer, which kills quickly. In his unvarying outfit of black mock turtleneck, Levi's blue jeans, dark socks, New Balance sneakers, and 1960s-style round spectacles, Jobs was fit and robust, his salt-and-pepper beard full and just a tiny bit bushy. Having turned 50 two years earlier, Jobs was on a tear. Apple had remade the music industry with the iPod and the iTunes music store. That year Jobs had sold his side project, Pixar, to Disney for $7.5 billion, making him the famed entertainment company's largest shareholder, a member of Disney's board of directors, and a billionaire several times over.

Jobs could see into the future better than anyone else in the technology industry. But four years later, after all

Apple accomplished between the first iPhone and the new model Jobs held in his hand, he refrained from asking Siri the existential question he knew was beyond its artificial intelligence yet of paramount importance: "What kind of company will Apple be after I'm gone?"

The death march that led to the iPhone was textbook Apple—favorites were played, key resources were diverted to a product that had captured the CEO's interest, the hours were brutal, yet the work felt important. Could another company with annual sales of $108 billion have achieved a similar feat in the same time frame? Probably not unless it had a CEO who believed that he could change the world and his company could put a "dent in the universe."

After his death at age fifty-six on October 5, 2011, Steve Jobs was rightly celebrated for his extraordinary contributions to the reordering of multiple industries. He revolutionized no fewer than four: computers, music (through the iTunes Store and the iPod), film (through Pixar, which pioneered computer animation), and communications (with the iPhone). Having helped define the computer industry as a young man, he was well on his way to ushering in its successor. Months before his death, at the triumphant debut of Apple's second iPad, Jobs declared the beginning of the "post-PC era"—meaning computing would no longer be confined to a desktop or laptop. In Apple, he oversaw a company whose products were world famous but whose methods were top secret.

Were Apple better understood, its fans and foes alike would see it as a giant jumble of contradictions, a company whose methods go against decades of well-established management maxims. It's as if Apple weren't paying attention to what they're teaching in business schools. In fact, it is not.

Apple is secretive at a time when the prevailing trend in business is toward transparency. Far from being empowered, its people operate within a narrow band of responsibility. Jobs famously encouraged the 2005 graduation class of Stanford not to "let the noise of others' opinions drown out your own inner voice, heart, and intuition." Yet Apple's own employees are expected to follow orders, not offer opinions. Good managers, we have been taught, delegate. Yet Apple's CEO was a micromanager in every sense of the word, from approving every ad his company created to deciding who would and wouldn't attend top-secret off-site meetings.

Apple flouts yet another piece of modern management's love of efficiency: It consistently leaves money on the table at a moment when profits are king and quarterly earnings exert a tyrannical sway over its fellow publicly traded companies. Apple, in fact, shows relatively little interest in Wall Street, seemingly viewing investors as an irritant at worst, a necessary evil at best. It aims to retain the vibrancy of a start-up at a time when many once-nimble tech companies (Microsoft, Yahoo!, AOL, and even Cisco come to mind) find ossification an inevitable side effect of growth.

Apple isn't even a particularly *nice* place to work in an era when legions of companies compete to be listed on *Fortune* magazine's annual ranking of most desirable workplaces. (Apple opts out of the competition altogether, choosing not to apply.) Then again, Apple clearly is doing something right. In fact, it has done little wrong since Steve Jobs returned to Cupertino in 1997. In the latter half of 2011, Apple and ExxonMobil jockeyed for position as the world's largest company by market capitalization.

If Apple is so good at what it does, just how does it do it anyway? Google's work environment has found its way into the popular culture. *Hey, I can go to work in my pajamas, eat Cap'n Crunch, and joust with the other engineers while atop my Razor scooter—wheeee!* Precious few have a clue what goes on at Apple when the camera isn't pointed at whichever executive is conducting a carefully rehearsed demo at an Apple product launch.

This is just how Apple wants it. As far as Apple is concerned, the subject of how it really works is taboo. Privately, executives refer to its playbook as the recipe for Apple's "secret sauce." Tim Cook, the longtime operations chief who became CEO in August 2011, six weeks before Steve Jobs died, once addressed the matter publicly. "That's a part of the magic of Apple," he said, when asked by a Wall Street analyst to comment on Apple's planning process. "And I don't want to let anybody know our magic because I don't want anybody copying it."

As for Apple's gadgets, as much as the world loves and admires them, few understand how Apple makes and markets them. It's a topic best grasped through an understanding of the nitty-gritty processes of working at Apple: how its leaders function, the way the company pits competing technology teams against one another, and its unique approach—or lack of an approach—to career development. While many members of Apple's middle ranks toil for years in the same exact role—yet another difference from the rest of the upward-and-onward corporate world—a handful of trusted lieutenants have bubbled up to become next-generation company leaders.

This book is an attempt to hack into Apple's closed world and to decode its secret systems so that aspiring entrepreneurs, curious middle managers, envious rival CEOs, and creatives who dream of turning insights into inventions can understand the company's processes and customs. If—and it's not a given—it were possible to imitate Apple, who wouldn't want to try? To confront that complicated task, the most logical place to start would be with Jobs. Jobs died at his Palo Alto home in 2011, but his spirit will inhabit Apple Inc. for years to come. To understand how Apple works is to know how his style was a refutation of the conventional wisdom of what a CEO should be.

Steven Paul Jobs changed the world, but he was the epitome of the hometown boy. In a paradox not unlike the many paradoxes of his company, Jobs was an urbane aesthete who nevertheless lived the life of a dyed-in-the-wool suburbanite. He professed a disdain for shopping malls, yet he put his company's first retail store in one. He drove to work every day of his adult life, the prototypical commuter more at home on the freeway than in a city center.

He was born in San Francisco in 1955. His adoptive parents moved the family first to Mountain View, and then Los Altos, both small towns in what was known at the time as the Santa Clara Valley. He attended high school in nearby Cupertino, and in some ways he never left. For brief periods he strayed from the sunny, arid strip between San Francisco and San Jose, an area where a collection of nascent defense-technology companies were replacing the apricot and prune orchards that dotted the landscape when Jobs was a boy. He briefly attended Reed College in Oregon, a liberal campus where the 1960s lingered well into the 1970s. Jobs camped out for a time on a friend's farm in Oregon, but when he needed money he came home to work for Atari. In these early years, he embraced strict vegetarianism, sampled a course on calligraphy—early evidence of a lifelong obsession with design—and sought to find himself in India. Again, he returned home. Years later, Jobs bought an apartment in the exclusive San Remo apartment building overlooking New York's Central Park. But the pull of lean-to buildings and the entrepreneurs who were creating companies in them proved strong: He never took up residence on the Upper West Side.

A cheerleader for what became known as Silicon Valley, Jobs would question the judgment of entrepreneurially minded people who advocated starting companies or furthering their careers anywhere else. Toward the beginning of his rejuvenation of Apple, in 1999, he belittled the former Disney executive Jeff Jordan for having graduated from Stanford University, "in the epicenter of entrepreneurship," and then leaving town for various positions. A decade later, Andy Miller, CEO and co-founder of Quattro Wireless, a mobile advertising company that Apple bought and whose technology became Apple's iAd, discussed geography with Jobs when the two met to hash out their deal. "Your company is in Waltham," Jobs said, mispronouncing the name of the Massachusetts town where Quattro was located. Miller tried correcting Jobs on the pronunciation, but Jobs cut him off. "I don't care,"

Jobs said. "You know what's in Waltham?" he asked, still mispronouncing the name. "Absolutely nothing."

The other titans of the tech industry immigrated to a place where Jobs was a native. Andy Grove of Intel was born in Hungary, Oracle co-founder Larry Ellison, in Chicago. Google's Larry Page and Sergey Brin hailed from Michigan and Russia, respectively. Mark Zuckerberg, the newest superstar of Silicon Valley when Jobs died, was born in suburban New York and founded Facebook in a Harvard dorm room. They all sought out the Silicon Valley that Jobs wove into his personal fabric at a young age. He loved to tell the story of phoning his neighbor, William Hewlett, to ask for spare parts for a device Jobs was building called a "frequency counter." He was thirteen years old. Hewlett, the co-founder of Hewlett-Packard, the original Silicon Valley company to start in a garage, gave Jobs the parts—and a summer job.

Jobs may have been of Silicon Valley, but he didn't always fit its stereotypes. He was savvy and knowledgeable about technology, but lacked formal training as an engineer. He was enough of a nerd to hang out at the Homebrew Computer Club with his friend Steve Wozniak, the personification of a 1970s propeller head. But Jobs was precocious: confident around women, a sharp dresser once he acquired some wealth (and before he began wearing the same clothes day in and day out), and a shrewd and demanding marketer and businessman. He was everything the engineers were not, yet he understood their technology well enough to tell them what products he wanted them to build for the consumers who would be his customers.

Apple began when Wozniak created the Apple I in

1976. Jobs had the gumption to realize that there was a broader market for the device, which "Woz" built mostly to impress his computer-club pals. The Apple II, released in 1977, sold so rapidly that Apple listed its shares on the Nasdaq stock exchange in 1980, making millionaires of the two young founders. As Apple grew, Woz quickly lost interest and Jobs dominated the company. He hired older men, including experienced Valley hands Mike Markkula and Mike Scott, and in 1983 the Pepsi executive John Sculley, to provide what Silicon Valley investors have long called "adult supervision."

Jobs oversaw the development of the Macintosh, a revolutionary computer in its time because it implemented the breakthrough technology Jobs had observed at nearby Xerox PARC, the photocopier company's Palo Alto research lab. With a computer "mouse" and a "graphical user interface" that allowed ordinary users to change sizes, fonts, and colors on their screens, the Mac changed the computer industry. When business faltered, however, Sculley kicked Jobs upstairs to the post of vice chairman. Jobs chose exile over sinecure, leaving Apple altogether in 1985.

Jobs's wilderness years were also some of his most important in terms of growth, professionally and personally. He founded NeXT, a high-end computer company initially targeted at education markets. It never gelled, but it gave him his first experience as a CEO. He'd gone from a mercurial screamer to a more nuanced developer of talent: Several of his top managers at NeXT formed the core of his eventual resuscitation of Apple. In 1986, he invested $10 million in a computer graphics company the filmmaker George Lucas owned that later would be called Pixar. After a decade of tinkering with different business models—Pixar for a time sold expensive workstation computers—the company would settle on computer-aided animation as its niche. Pixar was an "overnight" success when *Toy Story* debuted in 1995 and the company quickly went public, earning Jobs his second fortune.

It was also during his time away from Apple that Jobs transformed himself from a glamorous, if ascetic, bachelor—for a while he dated the singer Joan Baez and the writer Jennifer Egan—to a family man. After addressing a business school class at Stanford in 1990, he introduced himself to a student who had caught his eye, Laurene Powell. They married the next year and ultimately raised their three children on a quiet street in Palo Alto, not far from the Stanford campus. Once again, Jobs led a paradoxical life. A world-famous businessman at work, he lived in a home with no security, no gates, and no lawn: The grounds outside the Tudor house were covered with California poppies and apple trees. The neighbors all knew when Jobs was home, because his silver Mercedes SL55 AMG coupe would be parked in the driveway. Jobs succeeded in keeping his children, and his wife, for that matter, out of the public eye. Laurene Powell Jobs ran an education-oriented philanthropic organization and served on the board of Teach for America (with her husband's biographer, Walter Isaacson). A former investment banker, she spoke only occasionally in public. At the time of Jobs's death, their son, Reed, a Stanford undergraduate, lived next door with some friends in a house his parents bought after persuading a longtime neighbor to move down the block. That way Reed could be close to his ailing father, as well as his younger sisters, Erin and Eve.

Known for being alternately bullying and charming at

work, Jobs showed his neighbors the same combo package. Evelyn Richards, who lived around the block from Jobs, once sent her Girl Scout daughter to the Jobs household to sell cookies. "Jobs answered the door himself," Richards recalled. "But he told her he wouldn't buy any because cookies are sugary and bad for you." At the same time, his neighbors frequently spotted Jobs strolling around the neighborhood, either with his wife or, often, with his close friend and Apple board member Bill Campbell. Jobs also showed up at local gatherings just like everyone else. Richards recalled the Fourth of July block party in 2007, days after Apple began selling the iPhone, when Jobs showed off the phone to all who were interested. A poignant snapshot from that day shows Jobs out of uniform: He wore a baseball cap, a long-sleeved white shirt, and blue jeans, with a flannel shirt wrapped around his waist. In it, he stands next to another man, demonstrating the iPhone, looking like just any other Palo Alto dad displaying a new gizmo.

If power corrupts, then success enhances: It makes the qualities of a leader appear in sharp relief. As Jobs entered the last and mind-bogglingly productive phase of his career, the many paradoxes of his personality became the management systems of the company. This Jobs-ian transformation began in earnest in 1997.

The previous December, a floundering Apple had purchased NeXT. The prodigal co-founder returned as a "technical adviser," and NeXT's software became the foundation of a new operating system for Macintosh computers. The following July, Apple fired its CEO, Gil Amelio, a former chip executive from National Semiconductor who had failed to halt the hemorrhaging of cash that had begun under Apple's two previous CEOs, John Sculley and Michael Spindler.

Even good news at Apple highlighted the fallen icon's weaknesses. On August 6, 1997, Apple announced a $150 million investment from Microsoft. The cash certainly helped, but the real value to Apple was Microsoft's commitment to continue developing its Office productivity software for the Macintosh for at least five years. Apple was so diminished that summer that many software programs didn't come in a version for the Mac. The online publication CNET at the time opined that Microsoft's move "amounts to little more than good public relations." Microsoft, after all, didn't want Apple to die. The elimination of Apple would hurt Microsoft in the eyes of antitrust regulators. This same observer, a newsletter writer focused on Windows products, noted: "The investment still doesn't give Apple a coherent strategy for turning things around."

Behind the scenes, though, Jobs's turnaround plan was well under way. The next month, Apple announced that Jobs would become interim CEO of Apple until a suitable replacement could be found. It would be three years before Apple made Jobs the permanent CEO. Until then he was known around the company's headquarters as Apple's "iCEO," foreshadowing the i-nomenclature that would permeate Apple's branding. Interim or not, Jobs was busy putting the pieces into place for the company's rebirth. He recognized the importance of work Jonathan Ive was doing in Apple's design laboratory, and Jobs set Ive to work on what would become Apple's candy-colored iMacs—translucent, all-in-one computers that looked like clear TVs connected to a keyboard. He hired Tim Cook—an operations whiz from Compaq, and IBM before that—to revamp Apple's bloated and broken supply chain.

Then, with the company back on its feet thanks to the success of the iMac and the jettisoning of numerous unprofitable and non-core products, such as the hand-held Newton and printers that were indistinguishable from the competition, Jobs set Apple on the course that would transform it from niche pioneer to global cham-pion. Apple opened its first retail stores in 2001, initially to sell Macs. Then it started stocking the stores: with the first iPods that year, followed by a succession of follow-on iPods, including the Mini, the Nano, the Shuffle, and the Touch. Consumers used the iTunes Store, first introduced in 2003, to fill their devices with music, and later movies and TV shows. The stores were stuffed with Apple prod-ucts and scores of third-party accessories by 2010, when Apple released the groundbreaking iPad.

It was during this burst of creative energy that Apple's CEO first became ill. He learned in 2003 that he had a rare, initially treatable form of pancreatic cancer but didn't have the tumor removed until 2004, when he took his first leave of absence. A healthy period followed—this is when the iPhone was born and the iPad took shape—but Apple-watchers knew something was amiss when Jobs showed up for an Apple developers' conference in June 2008 looking gaunt. The next year he announced a sec-ond leave, this time so he could have a liver transplant performed. He returned to work in mid-2009 but never regained the weight he'd lost the previous year.

The last time Jobs presented to the public, on June 7,

2011, it was before the Cupertino City Council. He had come to show the city Apple's plans for a new, twelve-thousand-person headquarters and campus in Cupertino to be built partly on land purchased from a shrinking Hewlett-Packard. The hometown boy played to an awed audience, expressing his desire for his company to continue paying taxes in Cupertino and mindful of the history of the land in question. (Apple was Cupertino's largest taxpayer, he noted, and it would be a shame if the company were forced to move to Mountain View.) The presentation contained all the usual Jobs flourishes: clean slides, persuasive points to convince the council his plan was sound, and a dash of heartstring-pulling emotion. He noted that apricot trees had once covered the 150 acres where Hewlett-Packard had built its computer systems division. He knew this, of course, because he had grown up nearby. Now landscaping covered only 20 percent of the site, and too much of the rest was covered with asphalt. Apple's plans called for increasing the landscaping dramatically, including providing a home for six thousand trees where thirty-seven hundred now stood. "We've hired a senior arborist from Stanford," Jobs told the council—an expert in indigenous trees. Said the indigenous executive, who knew full well he wouldn't live to see the new headquarters built: "We'll want to plant some apricot trees."

When he died, much was made of how singular Steve Jobs had been. For comparisons, observers needed to reach back to the mythic inventors and showmen of earlier eras, particularly Thomas Edison and Walt Disney.

Jobs was singular, to be sure. But he also was of a type. He was what psychotherapist and business coach Michael Maccoby called a "productive narcissist."

In 2000, Maccoby published an insightful article in the *Harvard Business Review* that applies Freudian terminology to three categories of executives Maccoby had observed in corporate life. "Erotics" feel a need to be loved, value consensus, and as a result are not natural leaders. These are the people to whom a manager should assign tasks—and then heap praise for a job well done. "Obsessives" are by-the-books tacticians with a knack for making the trains run on time. An efficient head of logistics or bottom-line-oriented spreadsheet jockey is the classic obsessive. The greats of business history, however, are "productive narcissists," visionary risk takers with a burning desire to "change the world." Corporate narcissists are charismatic leaders willing to do whatever it takes to win and who couldn't give a fig about being liked.

Steve Jobs was the textbook example of a productive narcissist. An unimpressed Jobs was famous for calling other companies "bozos." His own executives endured their rides on what one called the "bozo/hero rollercoaster," often within the same marathon meeting. Jobs brought an artist's eye to the scientific world of computers. His paranoia built a company that is as secretive as the Central Intelligence Agency. Jobs, perhaps more than any other businessperson of the last century, created the future others couldn't see.

The way Jobs led is merely the first example (of many) of how Apple's ways depart from decades of received wisdom on corporate life. In his most recent book, *Great by Choice*, management expert Jim Collins and his co-author

Morten T. Hansen hold up Microsoft rather than Apple as the model of a company that delivers outstanding returns to shareholders. (It didn't help their analysis that the data set for the companies they investigated ended in 2002—shortly after Microsoft's star began to fade and just as Apple's began to shine.) For years, the trend in business has been toward empowerment. Collins rhapsodizes in his earlier classic *Good to Great* about the humble "Level 5 leader" who shares credit with his or her subordinates and delegates responsibility. In Collins's cosmology of corporate life, the reverse was supposed to be true as well. Great leaders weren't supposed to be tyrants. They were supposed to empathize with the feelings of those below them.

Jobs did just the opposite. He micromanaged to a shockingly high degree and to an amazingly low level in the organization. One ex-employee recalled being responsible for an email that would be sent to Apple customers simultaneously with the launch of a new version of a product. Ahead of the launch, Jobs engaged this employee in a repeated back-and-forth by email over the punctuation in the message. "A first iteration of anything was never good enough for him," said the former employee. At the height of his power Jobs personally ran marketing, oversaw product development, involved himself in the details of every acquisition, and met weekly with Apple's advertising agency. Before illness slowed him, Jobs was the only Apple executive to play a significant role at any Apple public event, be it a product launch or a keynote speech. When Apple did grant interviews to the press to promote an upcoming product launch, Jobs was the primary—and sometimes only—Apple spokesman.

There are few companies where this sort of leadership style would fly. But should there be? CEOs aren't supposed to be jerks. They're not supposed to make their
employees cry. They're not supposed to hog all the credit
for a team's job well done. Yet accepting that the flame
of one's own public profile needed to be extinguished at
the altar of Steve was a fact of life for even senior Apple
executives. Avie Tevanian, one of Apple's senior software
executives in the late 1990s and early 2000s, recalled the
time, in 2004, that he commented at a public event on
the expected upgrade cycle for the Mac operating system.
There was nothing controversial in what he said, in Tevanian's opinion. He merely was confirming what already
was well known, that the upgrade would take slightly
longer than prior releases. "I got a scathing phone call
from Steve," Tevanian remembered. "He said: 'Why would
you say something like that? We have no news to report;
you shouldn't have said that.'" Up to that point, Tevanian
hadn't spoken much in public, even though he was one
of the highest-ranking Apple executives. Afterward, he
rarely did at all, which was just the way Jobs wanted it.

Hogging the spotlight created resentment, but it was
also characteristic of the type of leader Jobs was. In his
book *The No Asshole Rule: Building a Civilized Workplace
and Surviving One That Isn't*, Stanford business professor
Robert Sutton calls Jobs "exhibit one" of chapter 6—titled
"The Virtues of Assholes"—a chapter Sutton said he didn't
want to write: "It sometimes seems as if his full name is
'Steve Jobs, that asshole.' I put 'Steve Jobs' and 'asshole' in
Google and got 89,400 matches."

Joking aside, Sutton goes on to make a case consistent with Maccoby's Freudian analysis. Perhaps, he argues,

ignoring the very qualities that adherents of "empowerment" have been advocating is an acceptable model of
leadership today. Jobs may have been an asshole, Sutton implies, but he was an effective asshole. People who
worked for Jobs argue, Sutton writes, that

> he is among the most imaginative, decisive and per-
> suasive people they've ever met. They admit that
> he inspires astounding effort and creativity from his
> people. And all suggest—although his tantrums and
> nasty critiques have driven the people around him
> crazy and driven many away—they are a crucial part
> of his success, especially his pursuit of perfection
> and relentless desire to make beautiful things. Even
> those who despise him most ask me, "So, doesn't
> Jobs prove that some assholes are worth the trouble?"

Jobs's insistence on involving himself in the smallest
of matters was as old as Apple itself. In his seminal book
about Apple's earliest days, *The Little Kingdom*, Michael
Moritz describes the lengths to which Jobs would go to
have things his way. "When an IBM salesman delivered
a blue Selectric typewriter instead of the neutral color he
had specified, Jobs erupted," Moritz wrote in 1984. "When
the phone company failed to install the ivory-colored
telephones Jobs had ordered, he complained until they
were changed." In the early days Jobs haggled with the
smallest of vendors, and typically in a less-than-congenial
or -respectful way. "He was very obnoxious to them,"
Gary Martin, an early Apple accountant, told Moritz. "He
had to get the lowest price they had. He'd call them on
the phone and say, 'That's not good enough. You better

sharpen your pencil.' We were all asking, 'How can you treat another human being like that?'"

A narcissist to be sure, Jobs also had obsessive traits, and he made sure the people below him obsessed about details as much as he did. Indeed, Jobs's requirement that things be done his way—and his persistence in verifying that his will be done—created Apple's obsessive culture and called to mind a domineering orchestra conductor. "The leadership structure at Apple is what allows Apple to thrive," recalled Michael Hailey, a former product marketing manager. "You had a visionary leader and people he trusted implicitly who had a knack for executing his vision. Jobs stayed involved from beginning to end to make sure everything matched his vision. He'd check off on the smallest things. That's how you get discipline."

Jobs was called Apple's editor and also a curator. He picked and chose from among the ideas his employees rigorously vetted before presenting to him. Over and over Apple employees who were exposed to the Jobs decision-making process voiced amazement at the CEO's uncanny knack for "being right." Frederick Van Johnson, an Apple marketer in the mid-2000s, described a typical Jobs reaction matrix to being presented with a product plan. "He'll look at it and he'll say, 'Yeah, great. Go for it.' He may say, 'That's crap, back to the drawing board. Why do you even work here?' Or he may say, 'That's great. But do this, this, and this, too.' Because he has that insight. You know, he's Steve. He may say, 'You know, people are really interested in seeing this kind of thing.' And you're like, how did you even know that? You're absolutely right. And it's not even blowing smoke. Normally, he has some sort of weird insight where he just knows."

How Jobs behaved as CEO will remain relevant at Apple for years because he so thoroughly infused the company with his idiosyncrasies. His unwillingness to follow other people's rules gave Apple employees license to ignore the rules of the people with whom they do business. Jobs's brutality in dealing with subordinates legitimized a frighteningly harsh, bullying, and demanding culture at Apple. Under Jobs, a culture of fear and intimidation found roots throughout the organization. If the narcissistic leader didn't care about being loved and was willing to take extraordinary risks in the interest of winning, then so would his subordinates. "High-performance teams should be at each other's throats" is how one person with relationships with multiple Apple executives summarized the culture. "You don't get to the right trade-off without each person advocating aggressively for his position." Arguments at Apple are personal and confrontational. This began at the top, and it is part of the company's culture.

The drubbing extended to anyone Jobs considered welcoming into the company. Jeff Jordan, a venture capitalist who held senior-level posts at eBay, PayPal, and start-up OpenTable, recalled Jobs's interviewing style when Jordan discussed a position at Pixar in 1999. Jobs invited Jordan, who had left Disney for a job at video retailer Hollywood Entertainment, to breakfast at Il Fornaio, a faux-rustic Italian eatery connected to the upscale Garden Court Hotel in downtown Palo Alto. Seated by himself in Il Fornaio's completely empty back room, Jordan waited for Jobs, who showed up late, wearing a T-shirt and washed-out cutoff shorts. "They sat him, and immediately placed three glasses of orange juice in front of him," said Jordan, who recounted the interview more than ten years later as the most memorable of his career. Jobs opened by insulting Jordan's professional accomplishments. "Disney's stores suck," he said. "They misrepresent my Pixar products all the time." Jordan defended himself by explaining why, in his opinion, Disney's stores did not suck, at which point Jobs abruptly changed gears. "After a bit, he leaned forward and said, 'Let me tell you about this position at Pixar.'" (Jobs famously played multiple angles; he called Jordan to talk about Pixar, but he also was snooping around for someone to run Apple's as-yet-unannounced retail stores.) Jordan began to grasp that he had witnessed a routine that was part theater and part genuine emotion. "His entire tone had changed at that point," said Jordan. "I realized it was just a complete stress test, a highly efficient winnowing process."

The rough treatment was a signature Jobs move. Another executive who interviewed with Jobs remembered his condescendingly challenging the assertion that Apple should sell music. This was a time when the iPod already was a modest success, but users lacked an easy way to buy songs. Jobs dismissed the idea during this executive's interview, but within months he announced the iTunes Music Store. Whether by pre-planned design or simply because it was his way, the confrontational interview questions allowed Jobs to learn if a recruit could handle Apple's rough culture. It would not be the last time the incoming employee would face a withering assault on his ideas.

Even during his ascetic days as a dope-smoking hippie in need of a shower, Steve Jobs exhibited the charismatic bearing around Apple that provoked comparisons not with Narcissus but with a messianic figure. Insiders referred to him merely as SJ. And as early as 1986, *Esquire* magazine titled a profile of Jobs in the wilderness of his new computer company, NeXT, as "The Second Coming of Steve Jobs." Journalist Alan Deutschman used the same trope as the title of his 2000 book, which chronicled the beginning of what truly became Apple's rebirth. The metaphor took hold even more firmly in later years. Anticipation of Apple's iPad was so intense in 2009 that bloggers began referring to the unreleased product as the "Jesus tablet." Following its release, the *Economist* ran an illustration of Jobs on its cover, caricaturing him as Jesus Christ, complete with a golden halo, under the headline: "Book of Jobs: Hope, Hype and Apple's iPad."

Jobs's spirit permeated Apple. Most big tech companies rely on massive acquisition programs to grow. Cisco, IBM, HP, and Oracle are the best examples. All are acquisitions machines. Apple, in stark contrast, has announced twelve acquisitions in the last decade, none exceeding $300 million in size. One reason is that the people who join through acquisitions haven't received the same inculcation as more carefully chosen employees. Given the challenges of integrating apostates and agnostics into a culture of true believers, Apple's CEO showed intense interest in each deal that did take place, even those that didn't tip any financial scales. Lars Albright, a co-founder and senior vice president for business development of Quattro Wireless, which Apple bought for $275 million in December 2009, recounted Jobs's role in what for Apple was a relatively small transaction. "Over time it became extremely clear that Steve was the voice of the company," said Albright. "We always thought it was something of a negotiating tactic for them to frequently say, 'We're going to check with Steve' or 'Steve has to weigh in.' But it turned out that at every major step he was briefed and giving opinions and setting the tone for the discussions."

The prelude to concluding a deal with Apple typically included an extended sit-down for the CEO of the target company with Jobs. The discussion had less to do with the strategic imperatives of the acquisition than it did with Jobs's attempts to feel out the talent he was acquiring. "There's a lot of Steve worshiping at the company," said an ex–Apple employee who joined by way of acquisition. "People will say, 'Well, Steve wants this, Steve wants that.' There are a lot of 'Steve' references in everyday life there. Some references are more relevant than others."

Some executives formalized the process of evoking the co-founder in written form. "The easiest way to get something done was to write an email with STEVE REQUEST in the subject line," said a former employee. "If you saw an email with a STEVE REQUEST at the top that would definitely get your attention." The result was a company that marched in lockstep with the perceived beat of a charismatic leader who was omnipresent. Said another former executive who joined Apple in an acquisition and stayed on for a while: "You can ask anyone in the company what Steve wants and you'll get an answer, even if 90 percent of them have never met Steve."

Apple employees liked to tell "Steve stories," such as tremulous rides in the elevator with him or staying out of his way if he appeared in the company cafeteria. Jobs himself used storytelling masterfully, and for years he used a parable—again, kind of like that other guy who "changed the world"—to drive home the message of accountability at Apple. According to more than one account, Jobs made a habit of delivering his parable to newly named vice presidents at Apple. Jobs would launch into a faux dialogue between himself and the janitor who cleans his office.

The scene begins with Jobs discovering an awkward situation whereby the waste bin in his office at Apple repeatedly is going unemptied. One day he happens to be working late and he directly confronts the janitor. "Why isn't my garbage being emptied," asks the powerful CEO. "Well, Mr. Jobs," replies the janitor, whose voice is quivering, "the locks have been changed and nobody gave me the new key." In his acting-out of the parable, Jobs is relieved to know there is an explanation to the mystery of his rotting trash and that there is an easy solution as well: Get the man a key.

At this point in his lesson, Jobs would shift to the moral that the newly minted VP—or, on occasion, a VP who needs to be reminded—was meant to take away from the parable. "When you're the janitor," Jobs would continue, now speaking directly to the executive, not theatrically to a fictional janitor, "reasons matter. Somewhere between the janitor and the CEO reasons stop mattering, and that Rubicon is crossed when you become a VP." Jobs made a practice of noting that if Apple were to repeatedly turn in a poor financial performance—it hadn't happened in years, of course—he would take the heat from Wall Street. VPs in turn would take the heat from him if their performance suffered. Finally, invoking Yoda from *Star Wars*, Jobs would tell the VP: "Do or do not. There is no try."

How long the deceased narcissistic co-founder, long-time CEO, and pervasive presence at Apple could continue to influence the corporate culture at Apple was Topic A among the media in the wake of Jobs's death. "Some of me is in the DNA of the company. But single-cell organisms aren't that interesting," Jobs said months before his death. "Apple is a complex multi-cellular organism." The whole look and feel of the company and its products reflect his personal aesthetic: simple, even austere, witty at times, and brutally efficient. But can an organization survive without its narcissistic driving force? Maccoby gives examples of companies that foundered, including Disney after Walt's death, and others that thrived, like IBM after the Watson family no longer ran it.

Two lines of inquiry address the dilemma of the indispensability of Steve Jobs. One is to look at what happened at Disney when the founder passed away (which I do in chapter 8). The other (which I'll look at in greater detail in chapter 9) is to see how Apple alumni who have left to start their own companies are faring.

Disney is an instructive example in pondering the influence Steve Jobs will continue to exert at Apple from his grave. In the years after his death, Disney execs were known to ask, "What would Walt do?" His office remained untouched for years, and in 1984, when Michael Eisner arrived as Disney's new chief executive, Walt's secretary was still on the job. Given the ubiquity of Jobs's presence at Apple when he was CEO, it's impossible to imagine that "What would Steve do?" won't be an oft-repeated phrase at Apple for quite some time. The degree to which Apple executives allow themselves to be driven by their interpretation of the answer to that question as opposed to doing what he taught them to do will in no small part determine the future success of the company. Indeed, his absence will put to the test a company culture that Jobs spent his final years attempting to institutionalize. It will take years, but eventually the world will learn if Steve Jobs *was* Apple—or if he succeeded in building a complex organism strong enough to survive his death.

2

Embrace Secrecy

Apple employees know something big is afoot when the carpenters appear in their office building. New walls are quickly erected. Doors are added and new security protocols put into place. Windows that once were transparent are now frosted. Other rooms have no windows at all. These are called lockdown rooms: No information goes in or out without a reason.

As an employee, the hubbub is disconcerting. You quite likely have no idea what is going on, and it's not like you're going to ask. If it hasn't been disclosed to you, then it's literally none of your business. What's more, your badge, which got you into particular areas before the new construction, no longer works there. All you can surmise is that a new, highly secretive project is under way, and you are not in the know. End of story.

Secrecy takes two basic forms at Apple—external and internal. There is the obvious kind, the secrecy that Apple uses as a way of keeping its products and practices hidden from competitors and the rest of the outside world. This cloaking device is the easier of the two types for the rank and file to understand because many companies try to keep their innovations under wraps. Internal secrecy, as evidenced by those mysterious walls and off-limits areas, is tougher to stomach. Yet the link between secrecy and productivity is another way that Apple challenges long-held management truths and the notion of transparency as a corporate virtue.

All companies have secrets, of course. The difference is that at Apple, everything is a secret. The company understands, by the way, that it takes things a little far, because it has the slightest hint of a sense of humor about its loose-lips-sink-ships mentality: A T-shirt for sale in the company store at 1 Infinite Loop, which is open to the public, reads: I VISITED THE APPLE CAMPUS. BUT THAT'S ALL I'M ALLOWED TO SAY.

Apple's airy physical surroundings contradict its secretive core. From above, it appears that an oval football stadium could be plopped down inside Infinite Loop. Yet Apple's headquarters isn't visible to the untrained eye. Interstate 280 runs along the north end of campus, but passersby wouldn't notice it as they sailed by at sixty-five miles an hour. (That wasn't always the case. In the late 1990s, Apple called attention to itself by hanging giant photographs of the likes of Albert Einstein and Amelia Earhart from the back of IL-3 as part of its "Think Different" campaign.) Visitors to the pulsing center of Apple's campus can drive around the loop that circles its six central buildings. Parking lots stand across from each of the main buildings, which are connected by walls and fences, forming a closed compound. Through the doors of those buildings, in the core of the loop, is a sunny, green courtyard with volleyball courts, grassy lawns, and outdoor seating for lunch. The splendid central cafeteria, Caffe Macs, features separate stations for fresh sushi, salad, and desserts and teems with Apple employees. They pay for their meals, by the way, unlike at Google, but the food is quite good and reasonably priced. A typical entrée might be grilled halibut on sautéed spinach with sweet potatoes—for $7. Other buildings across Apple's patchwork of real estate in Cupertino have their own restaurant-quality cafeterias.

The appearance is collegiate, but good luck auditing a class. Unlike Google's famously and ridiculously named "Googleplex," where a visitor can roam the inner courtyards and slip into an open door as employees come and go, Apple's buildings are airtight. Employees can be spotted on the volleyball courts from time to time. More typically, visitors gaping into the courtyard will see a campus in constant motion. Apple employees scurry from building to building for meetings that start and end on time.

Inside, Apple's offices are decorated in corporate drab. The office of the CEO and boardroom are on the fourth floor of IL-1. Other Apple buildings—some rented, some owned—fan out around the Infinite Loop cluster in a checkerboard fashion because Apple doesn't control every building in the neighborhood. These other buildings carry the name of the streets on which they sit, like Mariani 1 and DeAnza 12.

For new recruits, the secret keeping begins even before they learn which of these buildings they'll be working in. Despite surviving multiple rounds of rigorous interviews,

many employees are hired into so-called dummy positions, roles that aren't explained in detail until after they
join the company. The new hires have been welcomed
but not yet indoctrinated and aren't necessarily to be
trusted with information as sensitive as their own mission. "They wouldn't tell me what it was," remembered a
former engineer who had been a graduate student before
joining Apple. "I knew it was related to the iPod, but not
what the job was." Others do know but won't say, a realization that hits the newbies on their first day of work at
new-employee orientation.

"You sit down, and you start with the usual roundtable
of who is doing what," recalled Bob Borchers, a product
marketing executive in the early days of the iPhone. "And
half the folks can't tell you what they're doing, because it's
a secret project that they've gotten hired for."

The new employees learn that first day of work that
they've joined a different kind of company than anywhere
they've worked before. Outside, Apple is revered. Inside,
it is cultish, and neophytes are only entrusted with so
much information. All new employees attend a half day
of orientation, always on a Monday—unless Monday is a
holiday. Much of the orientation is standard big-company
stuff: a welcome package with stickers saying you've
joined Apple, HR forms, and the like, as well as a T-shirt
that says CLASS OF with the current year emblazoned on the
front. Apple quickly makes the employees of the relatively
few companies it acquires understand they are now part
of the Apple family. Lars Albright, who became director
of partnerships and alliances in Apple's iAd mobile advertising business when Apple bought his start-up, Quattro
Wireless, recalled the delight when a bevy of shiny new

iMacs showed up almost immediately following the close of the transaction: "People felt very quickly like you were part of something special," he said. Orientation Monday brings another rare treat. "There's only one free lunch at Apple, and it's on your first day," said a former employee.

Another highlight of an employee's first day at Apple is the realization that there's no one to help you connect your newly issued computer. The assumption is that those smart enough and tech-savvy enough to be hired at Apple can hook themselves up to the network. "Most people are expected to be able to connect to servers," said an Apple observer. "People say: 'That shit was hard, but I figured out who to talk to.' That's super smart. It's a clever way to get people to connect with each other."

Apple does toss one bone to new recruits. An informal "iBuddy" system provides the name of a peer outside the primary team who can serve as a sounding board, someone for the bewildered new employee to ask questions. Many have said they met with their iBuddy once or twice at the beginning of their tenure—before they became too busy to meet again.

Reality sets in at orientation in the form of the security briefing, the one element that no Apple employee forgets. Call it Scared Silent. Borchers, the iPhone marketing executive who had worked at Nike and Nokia before joining Apple, recalled the scene. "Whoever headed up security came in and said, 'Okay, everybody understands secrecy and security are incredibly important here. Let me just explain why.' And the rationale is that when Apple launches a product, if it's been a secret up until the launch, the amount of press and coverage and buzz that you get is hugely valuable to the company. 'It's worth millions of dollars,' I remember her saying." So there's no confusion, the penalty for revealing Apple secrets, intentionally or unintentionally, is clear: swift termination.

The aversion to pre-release publicity is a constant at Apple. Phil Schiller, Apple's powerful senior vice president of product marketing, has been known to compare an Apple product launch to a blockbuster Hollywood movie debut. There is tremendous emphasis on the product's first few days, akin to a film's opening weekend. Releasing details ahead of time would dampen the anticipation. Indeed, Apple "fanboys" camp out in front of Apple stores in anticipation of new Apple product releases in a way that is reminiscent of the lines that once greeted a new installment in the *Lord of the Rings* or *Star Wars* franchises.

This is precisely the effect Schiller desires from the Day One burst of activity. "I still remember him drawing the spike over and over," said a former Apple executive who worked in Schiller's organization. The analogy doesn't translate perfectly, of course. Hollywood plays trailers assiduously in multiple venues in order to stoke demand. Apple's equivalent is the rumor mill, which anticipates new products, thus providing pre-release publicity free of charge.

Another reason why Apple wants new products to remain in stealth mode until their release dates is so they don't steal the thunder from existing products. If consumers know exactly what's coming, they may hold off on a purchase for fear it will be superseded by the next generation. This dulling of demand renders products already on retail shelves or in warehouses awaiting purchase worthless. (Indeed, even imperfect information can damage sales: Apple said expectations of a new iPhone in the summer of 2011 hurt sales of the existing iPhone 4.)

Most important, announcing products before they are ready gives the competition time to respond, raises customer expectations, and opens a company up to the carping of critics who are bashing an idea rather than an actual product. Companies who fail to grasp the power of secrecy do so at their peril. Hewlett-Packard committed this product marketing sin in early 2011 by announcing it would have an ill-defined "cloud" offering later in the year. Unfathomably, HP later "pre-announced" the sale of its PC business, inflicting immeasurable damage on a unit that accounted for nearly a third of its sales. (HP's board fired its CEO, Léo Apotheker, shortly after the announcement about the PC unit.)

Apple secrecy over its product launches is extraordinary largely because so few other companies keep secrets nearly as well. Matt Drance worked at Apple for eight years, first as an engineer, and then as an "evangelist" helping outside developers design products for the Apple platform. He looked on in amazement at the non-Apple approach. "Here's a shocker," he wrote on his blog, *Apple Outsider*, after Korean phone maker LG embarrassingly blew an announced product deadline for a new smartphone.

The product you send out the door will probably come later, and with fewer features, than you intended. Time runs out. Unexpected complications arise. Bugs overwhelm the team. Your partner invalidates your plans. Something's got to give.

You need to either take something out, or wait longer. But if you've spent months blowing smoke,
now *everyone* is waiting longer. The problem with
talking smack is you immediately put yourself on
the clock. You almost guarantee public disappointment when the product does not ship as (or when)
promised. If you just shut your mouth and let the
product speak for itself—once you actually *have*
a product—then there's a much better chance for
people to be pleasantly surprised. Some companies
understand this. Others clearly do not.

Secrecy at Apple is strictly enforced from within. Valley
engineers love to swap stories about their work, but Apple
engineers have a reputation for keeping to themselves.
"I've had friends who've been reprimanded for talking too
much," reported a former engineer. "It's best in general
not to talk about work." The mentality makes Apple stand
out in the tech world. "Fear is palpable there, including
among partners," said Gina Bianchini, a seasoned Valley
entrepreneur and longtime Apple watcher who is CEO of
Mightybell.com, an Internet start-up. (The home page of
Mightybell.com wryly states "Handmade in California,"
an homage to the bigger company's tagline "Designed
by Apple in California.") "No company has that level of
fear." In 2011, she explained Apple's outsider status with
an epiphany from TED, an annual tech-industry think-
fest in Long Beach, California, attended by a who's who
of top executives and investors. "One thing I observed
this year at TED: The Apple employee population does
not circulate within the Silicon Valley ecosystem. Nobody
knows anybody at Apple. The Internet people all know

each other, but Apple lives in its own world. Inside, every-one is so afraid to talk that it's easier to mix exclusively with each other."

Another Valley engineer plays in a regular poker game with a team of Apple employees. The understanding is that if Apple comes up at the card table, the subject will be changed. Being fired for blabbing is a well-founded concern. For example, people working on launch events will be given watermarked paper copies of a booklet called *Rules of the Road* that details every milestone lead-ing up to launch day. In the booklet is a legal statement whose message is clear: If this copy ends up in the wrong hands, the responsible party will be fired.

Apple goes to great lengths to maintain discipline. "There were just these things that were kept very, very secret," said a former senior executive. "There was a proj-ect we were working on, where we put in special locks on one of the floors and put up a couple of extra doors to hide away a team that was working on stuff. You had to sign extra-special agreements acknowledging that you were working on a super-secret project and you wouldn't talk about it to anyone—not your wife, not your kids."

The stress from such secret keeping becomes too much for some. Jobs made a habit of personally conveying to employees the confidentiality of all-company broadcasts. Recalled one ex-employee: "He'd say, 'Anything disclosed from this meeting will result not just in termination but in the prosecution to the fullest extent that our lawyers can.' This made me very uncomfortable. You have to watch everything you do. I'd have nightmares."

Visitors are allowed at Apple offices, but they are kept under tight wraps. Some report being shocked at the

unwillingness of employees to leave their guests unat-
tended for even a few moments in the cafeteria. A tech-
industry executive visiting a friend in mid-2011 was asked
not to post anything to Twitter about the visit or to "check
in" at the popular website Foursquare, which publishes a
user's location. In Apple's view of the world, simply revealing that someone visited Apple on undisclosed business
could lead to divulging something about Apple's agenda.
(One wonders if Apple will discourage the use of its "Find
My Friends" feature, added to the iPhone's software in late
2011, a feature the company described as a "temporary
location-sharing" service.)

For the most part, Apple counts on its employees to
censor themselves. But in some cases, it pays attention
to what employees say when they are out of the office—
even when they've only walked across the street for a
beer. BJ's Restaurant and Brewhouse is tucked so close
to Apple's Cupertino campus that insiders jokingly refer
to it as IL-7, for "Infinite Loop 7," a building that doesn't
exist. Company lore holds that plainclothes Apple security
agents lurk near the bar at BJ's and that employees have
been fired for loose talk there. It doesn't quite matter if
the yarn is true or apocryphal. The fact that employees
repeat it serves the purpose.

Steve Jobs once said that not talking about the inner
workings of the company is something he borrowed from
Walt Disney. The creator of the original Magic Kingdom
felt the magic the public attributed to Disney would be
diminished by excessive focus on what went on behind
the scenes. What's more, Disney enforced strict internal

secrecy. When it was planning Walt Disney World in Flor-
ida in the 1960s, for example, Disney formed a committee
to work on a "Project X." Internal memos about the plans
for the new theme park were numbered so they could be
tracked, according to Neal Gabler's exhaustive biography,
Walt Disney: The Triumph of the American Imagination.

It's one thing to pressure employees to keep information from falling into the wrong hands. Apple's twist
is that those wrong hands happen to include one's own
colleagues. It is, in the words of one former employee,
"the ultimate need-to-know culture." Teams are purposely
kept apart, sometimes because they are unknowingly
competing against one another, but more often because
the Apple way is to mind one's own business. This has
a side benefit that is striking in its simplicity: Employees kept from butting into one another's affairs will have
more time to focus on their own work. Below a certain
level, it is difficult to play politics at Apple, because the
average employee doesn't have enough information to get
into the game. Like a horse fitted with blinders, the Apple
employee charges forward to the exclusion of all else.

Apple created an elaborate and unnerving system to
enforce internal secrecy. It revolves around the concept
of disclosure. To discuss a topic at a meeting, one must
be sure everyone in the room is "disclosed" on the topic,
meaning they have been made privy to certain secrets.
"You can't talk about any secret until you're sure everyone is disclosed on it," said an ex-employee. As a result,
Apple employees and their projects are pieces of a puzzle.
The snapshot of the completed puzzle is known only at
the highest reaches of the organization. It calls to mind
the cells a resistance organization plants behind enemy

lines, whose members aren't given information that could incriminate a comrade. Jon Rubinstein, formerly Apple's senior hardware executive, once deployed the comparison in a less flattering but equally effective manner. "We have cells, like a terrorist organization," he told *Businessweek* in 2000. "Everything is on a need-to-know basis."

As with any secret society, trustworthiness is not assumed. New additions to a group are kept out of the loop for a period of time, at least until they have earned their manager's trust. Employees tell stories of working on "core technology" rather than actual products or of not being allowed to sit near the rest of the group for a months-long probation period. Organization charts, typical fare at most big companies, don't exist at Apple. That is information employees don't need and outsiders shouldn't have. (When *Fortune* magazine printed an Apple org chart of its own design in May 2011, visitors to Apple told tales of employees becoming nervous merely being seen with a printed copy of it on their desks.) Employees do have one important source of information, however: the internal Apple Directory. This electronic guide lists each employee's name, group, manager, location, email, and phone number, and might include a photograph.

Apple employees don't need an organization chart to know who is powerful, of course. The executive team, a small council of advisers to the CEO, runs the company, assisted by a cadre of fewer than one hundred vice presidents. But rank doesn't always confer status at Apple. Everyone is aware of an unwritten caste system. The industrial designers are untouchable, as were, until his death, a tiny group of engineers who had worked with Steve Jobs for years, some dating to his first stint at Apple. A small group of engineers carries the title of DEST, distinguished engineer/scientist, technologist. These are individual contributors with clout in the organization but no management responsibilities. Otherwise, status fluctuates with the prominence of the products on which one works. As the success of the iPhone and iPad grew, the coolest faction of the company was the software engineers working on Apple's mobile operating system software, known as iOS. Hardware engineers and, grudgingly, product marketers connected with the devices ranked high in the pecking order, followed by people in the iTunes, iCloud, and other online services organizations. Employees associated primarily with the Macintosh, once the cocks of the roost, were considered second-rate in the Apple hierarchy by this time. In terms of corporate coolness, functions such as sales, human resources, and customer service wouldn't even rate.

With silos being the norm at Apple, the surprise is the silos within silos. "There are no open doors at Apple," said one former employee. Security badges allow an employee into only certain areas, and it isn't uncommon for employees to be able to go places their boss cannot. Some areas are even more secretive than others, and this has nothing to do with special projects. An example is the famous industrial design lab where Apple's designers work. So restrictive is the access to the lab that few Apple employees have ever seen inside its doors.

In his best-selling book *Incognito*, neuroscientist David Eagleman writes about the deleterious impact of a culture of secrecy. "The main thing to know about secrets," he says, "is that keeping them is unhealthy for the brain."

People want to tell secrets, he explained, and have a strong natural tendency to do so. Apple solves this problem by keeping its employees in the dark as much as possible. But it also begs the question of the happiness of Apple employees.

By and large, Apple is a collaborative and cooperative environment, devoid of overt politicking. The reason for the cooperation, according to former insiders, is the command-and-control structure. "Everyone knows that seamless integration between the various parts is key to making the magic happen," according to Rob Schoeben, a former vice president who oversaw product marketing for software applications. "At Apple, teams work together constantly. Steve will rip your nuts off if you didn't," he said while Jobs was still alive. Under Bill Gates, Microsoft had a reputation for being a political infighting nightmare, the implication being that Gates liked the results of the survival-of-the-fittest mentality.

Apple's culture may be cooperative, but it isn't usually nice, and it's almost never relaxed. "When you're on the campus, you never get the feeling that people are slacking off," said an observer with access to Apple's upper ranks. "The fighting can get personal and ugly. There's a mentality that it's okay to shred somebody in the spirit of making the best products." Apple's high standards come into play. "The pressure to be perfect is the overriding concern," said one ex-executive. "And it's hard to be perfect." Another former insider described the all-too-common stories executives told of having personal time off ruined because of an urgent "Steve request." "They went like this: 'On vacation my product was going to be in a keynote, and I had to jump on a plane and rehearse all weekend.'"

The competitive nature of the Apple culture comes into play. "Apple is a prizefight every day you go to work," said Steve Doil, a onetime executive in Apple's supply-chain organization. "If you're distracted even a little bit then you slow down the team." A former executive described the Apple culture in similar terms. "It's a culture of excellence," this executive noted. "There's a sense that you have to play your very best game. You don't want to be the weak link. There is an intense desire to not let the company down. Everybody has worked so hard and is so dedicated."

Apple's culture is the polar opposite of Google's, where flyers announcing extracurricular activities—from ski outings to a high-profile author series—hang everywhere. At Apple, the iTunes team sponsors the occasional band, and there is a company gym (which isn't free), but by and large Apple people come to work to work. "At meetings, there is no discussion about the lake house where you just spent the weekend," recalled a senior engineer. "You get right down to business." The contrast with the non-Apple world is stark. "When you interact with people at other companies, there's just a relative lack of intensity," said this engineer. "At Apple, people are so committed that they go home at night and don't leave Apple behind them. What they do at Apple is their true religion."

The attitude toward work at Apple hasn't changed over the decades. Here's how Joe Nocera, writing in *Esquire* magazine in 1986, described Jobs's perspective on the Apple work environment:

> He used to talk, for instance, about making Apple an "insanely great" place to work, but he wasn't talking about irresistible perks or liberal benefits.

Instead, he was talking about creating an environment where you would work harder and longer than you'd ever worked in your life, under the most grinding of deadline pressure, with more responsibility than you ever thought you could handle, never taking vacations, rarely getting even a weekend off…and you wouldn't care! You'd love it! You'd get to the point where you couldn't live without the work and the responsibility and the grinding deadline pressure. All of the people in this room had known such feelings about work—feelings that were exhilarating and personal and even intimate—and they'd known them while working for Steve Jobs. They all shared a private history of their work together at Apple. It was their bond, and no one who was not there could ever fully understand it.

Almost nobody describes working at Apple as being fun. In fact, when asked if Apple is a "fun" place, the responses are remarkably consistent. "People are incredibly passionate about the great stuff they are working on," said one former employee. "There is not a culture of recognizing and celebrating success. It's very much about work." Said another: "If you're a die-hard Apple geek, it's magical. It's also a really tough place to work. You have products that go from inception to launch, which means really late hours." A third similarly dodged the question: "Because people are so passionate about Apple, they are aligned with the mission of the company."

If they don't join for a good time, they also don't join Apple for the money. Sure Apple has spawned its share of stock-options millionaires—particularly those who had the good timing to join in the first five or so years after Jobs returned. "You can get paid a lot of money at most places here in the Valley," said Frederick Van Johnson, the former Apple marketing employee. "Money is not the metric."

By reputation, Apple pays salaries that are competitive with the marketplace—but no better. A senior director might make an annual salary of $200,000 with bonuses in good years amounting to 50 percent of the base. Talking about money is frowned upon at Apple. "I think working at a company like that, and actually being passionate about making cool things, is cool," said Johnson, summarizing the ethos. "Sitting in a bar and seeing that 90 percent of the people there are using devices that your company made...there is something cool about that, and you can't put a dollar value on it."

Steve Jobs—who was famously uninterested in discussing money—took a nuanced view of the subject of happiness and enjoyment at Apple. "I don't know anyone who wouldn't say it's the most fulfilling experience in their lives," he said. "People love it, which is different than saying they have fun. Fun comes and goes."

3

Focus Obsessively

Tucked away in a walled-off section of the creative studio of Apple's main marketing building is a room devoted to packaging. Compared with weighty and complex tasks such as software design or hardware manufacturing, packaging would be a pedestrian concern at many companies, almost an afterthought. Not at Apple, which devotes tremendous energy and resources to how it wraps its products. The packaging room is so secure that those with access to it need to badge in and out. To fully grasp how seriously Apple executives sweat the small stuff, consider this: For months, a packaging designer was holed up in this room performing the most mundane of tasks— opening boxes.

Mundane, perhaps, but also critically important. Inside the covert lab were hundreds of iPod box prototypes. That's right: hundreds of boxes whose sole function was to give the designer the ability to experience the moment when customers picked up and held their new toy for the first time. One after another, the designer created and tested an endless series of arrows, colors, and tapes for a tiny tab designed to show the consumer where to pull back the invisible, full-bleed sticker adhered to the top of the clear iPod box. Getting it just right was this particular designer's obsession. What's more, it wasn't just about one box. The tabs were placed so that when Apple's factory packed multiple boxes for shipping to retail stores, there was a natural negative space between the boxes that protected and preserved the tab.

How a customer opens a box must be one of the last things a typical product designer would consider. Yet for Apple, the inexpensive box merits as much attention as the high-margin electronic device inside. As the last thing customers see before their greatly anticipated device, Apple's packages are the capstone to a highly honed and exceedingly expensive process. It begins with prototype design, progresses to a collaboration between supply-chain experts who source the components and product managers who coordinate the assembly of hardware and software, and ends with a coordinated marketing, pricing, and retailing plan to get the devices in consumers' hands.

Anticipating how the customer will feel holding a simple white box is merely the culmination of many thousands of details Apple will have thought of along the way. "Attention to detail, to me, symbolizes that you really care about the user, all the way through," said Deep Nishar, an early Google executive who leads user-interface design for the Web company LinkedIn. Nishar described the reverence some of the designers who work for him have for the box that held their first iPhone. "Do you remember the packaging it came in?" he asked. "Some of them have kept it on their shelves. For the first time in history it was a spring-loaded box. It opened slowly. It continued to evoke that emotion and that feeling of anticipation, that you are about to see something beautiful, something great, something you had been reading about and hearing about, and had watched Steve talk about and demo. That's the attention to detail, the feeling you want to invoke."

Obsessing over details and bringing a Buddhist level of focus to a narrow assortment of offerings sets Apple apart from its competitors. Buddhism—a faith Jobs studied intensely—teaches that if you are going to prepare a cup of tea, the making of the cup of tea should command all your attention; even this insignificant task should be completed with all the mastery you can bring to it. It's a seemingly goofy spiritual idea that can pay great dividends in the corporate world. Well-designed products provide their manufacturers with enviable benefits internally and externally. Internally, talent and resources flow to the products that the company does best.

Externally, good design subliminally telegraphs to consumers that the manufacturer cares about them. This, in turn, creates a bond between brand and consumer that transcends price points. *I can't wait to get the new iPad* versus *Which is a better deal, a Kindle or a Nook?* So how does Apple use focus to set itself apart when it comes to design, manufacturing, and corporate planning?

Evoking a *feeling* is an extraordinary act for a device maker, let alone a packaging designer working for a device maker. (Try to imagine a Dell laptop evoking a feeling of any kind, other than frustration.) Yet it is what Steve Jobs did at Apple from the day he started the company. Jobs refused to think of Apple's devices in a conventional way. They weren't gadgets; they were works of art. "I think the artistry is in having an insight into what one sees around them," he said in a 1995 interview for the Computerworld Smithsonian Awards Program Oral History Project. Jobs was referring to the people he had hired at Apple in its early days. Their goal, he said, was

> putting things together in a way no one else has before and finding a way to express that to other people who don't have that insight so they can get some of the advantage of that insight that makes them feel a certain way or allows them to do a certain thing. If you study these people a little bit more what you'll find is that in this particular time, in the 70s and the 80s, the best people in computers would have normally been poets and writers and musicians. Almost all of them were musicians. A lot of them were poets on the side. They went into computers because it was so compelling. It was fresh and new. It was a new medium of expression for their creative talents. The feelings and the passion that people put into it were completely indistinguishable from a poet or a painter.

In retrospect, it seems almost hubristic for Jobs to have compared computer designers—or, heaven forbid, *cardboard-box* designers—to artists. It's yet another topic that would seem a bit hokey, or even fringe, if the backdrop were some other company. When an approach to creating gadgets enters the cultural zeitgeist, however, and when awareness of that approach leads to customers snapping up so much product that the company in question blossoms into the most richly valued company in the world, the poetry of consumer electronics rises to the stature of its circuitry.

Apple is different, and what always has set Apple apart is its approach to products. Whether Jobs was describing the typical early Apple employee or merely talking elliptically about himself, Apple fashioned itself early on as a renegade. In the early days, Jobs famously flew a pirate's skull-and-crossbones banner above the building that housed the Macintosh team, which he oversaw. From the beginning, Apple stood apart from the rest of the computer industry. The ethos at Apple was always about its uniqueness, and attention to detail is part of that ethos.

The computer industry was about standardization. "Clones" of IBM PCs were one of the industry's great innovations. Apple, with its devotion to superior computers, was briefly an icon, but mostly it was a niche player. Years later, when Hewlett-Packard was enduring one of its many crises, a well-placed Silicon Valley executive reflected on why it would be difficult even for a talented Apple executive to turn HP around. "When Steve came back to Apple morale was terrible, but there remained a culture that understood what it meant to make great products," this executive said. "HP hasn't had that in years. There wouldn't be anyone there to lead."

The genesis of most Apple products is simply Apple's desire to make them. Not focus groups. Not reader surveys. Not a competitive analysis. An unwillingness to stick a finger in the wind of customer requirements was one of Steve Jobs's favorite tropes over the years. "When we first started Apple we really built the first computer because we wanted one," he told Michael Moritz in the early 1980s for his book *The Little Kingdom*. It was a line that Jobs repeated over and over for decades. Twenty-five years later he stated, "We really do have the strong belief that we are building products for ourselves."

The iPhone is a classic case in point. Prior to the device's introduction, Apple executives typically hated their smartphones. "That's why we decided to do our own," Jobs said in an explanation that works at two levels: It's undoubtedly true, but it also sends a compelling message to customers. *We like the dog food so much we eat it ourselves. You won't be disappointed.*

It's astounding how little has changed philosophically at Apple from its earliest days to the present. Speaking of Jobs, Moritz writes: "He was unwilling to let product planning become burdened with analysis, focus groups, decision trees, the shifts of the bell curve, or any of the painful drudgery he associated with large companies. He found Apple's prototype customer in the mirror and the company came to develop computers that Jobs, at one time or another, decided he would like to own."

Design is the most tangible way to see Apple's focus on detail. Apple products are born in another highly secured lab accessible to only a tiny number of Apple employees. It is called the Industrial Design studio, or ID for short. Its master is the designer Jonathan Ive, the closest any Apple executive other than Steve Jobs has ever come to celebrity status. Jobs loved spending time in the design studio, where he would sample the cookie dough Ive and his team were mixing.

The key to Apple's design philosophy is that design is where Apple products start. Competitors marvel at the point of prominence Apple's industrial designers have. "Most companies make all their plans, all their marketing, all their positioning, and then they kind of hand it down to a designer," said Yves Behar, CEO of the design consultancy Fuseproject. The process is reversed at Apple, where everyone else in the organization needs to conform to the designer's vision. "If the designers say the material has to have integrity, the whole organization says okay," said Behar. In other words, a designer typically would be told what to do and say by the folks in manufacturing. At Apple it works the other way around.

John Sculley, Apple's CEO in the 1980s, has continued to pay close attention to Apple, despite having had no relationship with the company in years. "Everything at Apple can be best understood through the lens of designing," he told Leander Kahney, editor of the Apple-focused blog *Cult of Mac*, in 2010. He related a recent story about a friend who held meetings at Apple and Microsoft on the same day. "He went into the meeting at Apple [and] as soon as the designers walked in the room, everyone stopped talking because the designers are the most respected people in the organization. It is only at Apple where design reports directly to the CEO. Later in the day he was at Microsoft. When he went into the Microsoft meeting, everybody was talking and then the meeting starts and no designers ever walk into the room. All the technical people are sitting there trying to add their ideas of what ought to be in the design. That's a recipe for disaster."

Once the design is under way, the rest of the company kicks into gear. The two organizations that will be responsible for the product are the supply-chain team and the engineering corps. Thus begins the Apple New Product Process, or ANPP. The ANPP is the step-by-step playbook spelling out everything that needs to get done to make the product. The ANPP wasn't always unique to Apple. Xerox, HP, and others used a similar playbook in the late 1970s and early 1980s. A former Apple engineer described Apple's process, which began as a manufacturing aid for the Macintosh, as part art, part science. The goal of the ANPP "is to automate the science part so you can focus on the art," said this engineer. The process elaborately maps out the stages a product's creation will follow, who touches it, how responsibilities will be assigned across functions, and when assignments will be completed.

When a product is ready to leave the lab, two key people will take control: an engineering program manager, or EPM, and a global supply manager, or GSM. The former dictates what the product should be, and coordinates the work of teams of engineers. So powerful and feared are the program managers that some refer to them as the "EPM mafia." The global supply manager, working on the operations group that Tim Cook built, figures out how to get the materials to make it. They do everything from sourcing to procurement to overseeing production. The two sides collaborate, sometimes with tension. "The way you end any discussion at Apple is: 'It's the right thing for the product.' If you bring the data that proves that, you win," said an engineer from the mid-2000s.

EPMs and GSMs at Apple are based in Cupertino, but they spend much of their time in China, where Apple contracts with Chinese manufacturers to build its computers and mobile devices. Other companies will attempt to perfect design and then outsource the manufacturing. This is the most cost-effective way. Apple takes an approach that often is the least cost-effective. It, too, designs products to be built and then tested at outsourced manufacturing sites. But once Apple is done designing, building, and testing a product it starts designing, building, and testing all over again. This "overt rhythm," in the words of a former Apple engineer, culminates every four to six weeks with a gathering of key employees at a factory in China. An engineering program manager, whose job it is to pull together the various hardware and software engineers who contribute to a product, will typically bring the latest beta version back to Cupertino for senior executives to see—and then get right back on a plane for China to repeat the process.

Integration is the key. Steve Jobs summarized Apple's approach in an interview published in *Fortune* in 2008. "You can't do what you can do at Apple anywhere else," he said. "The engineering is long gone in most PC companies. In the consumer-electronics companies, they don't understand the software parts of it. And so you really can't make the products that you can make at Apple anywhere else right now. Apple's the only company that has everything under one roof. There's no other company that could make a MacBook Air and the reason is that not only do we control the hardware, but we control the operating system. And it is the intimate interaction between the operating system and the hardware that allows us to do that." Jobs was speaking at a conceptual level. A former Apple engineer broke it down to the nitty-gritty: "Apple is all about integration. The way to get true integration is to control everything from the operating system down to what kind of saw you are going to use on the glass."

Think about that for a moment, because it's not an exaggeration. Apple doesn't own the saw, and it doesn't own the company that owns the saw. It also doesn't staff the factory where the saw will be used. But it absolutely has an opinion as to which saw its supplier will use. It's a new form of vertical integration. Where once a manufacturer would own every step of the process, Apple now controls each step without owning any of it.

Integration is also internal at Apple. "Apple is not dependent on other companies to turn its vision into products," said Rob Schoeben, a former top product marketing executive. "Microsoft was always frustrated that the PC industry didn't do a better job of making PCs. Vertical integration is such a huge advantage for Apple. It's shocking that no one has replicated it." It's possible Apple's approach hasn't been replicated because so few companies are organized the way Apple is.

As interesting as it is to understand why Apple chooses to make what it makes, it is equally insightful to study what it decides *not* to make. Saying no is a core tenet of Apple product development and, for that matter, Apple's approach to doing business. In fact, the ability to say no— to reject features, products, categories, market segments, deals, and even certain partners—is how Steve Jobs explained Apple's core strengths. "Focusing is powerful," he said. "A start-up's focus is very clear. Focus is not saying yes. It is saying no to really great ideas."

Jobs preached this message inside Apple. It's worth noting that he is not the first to have this insight. The observation more typically comes from those in the aesthetic rather than the entrepreneurial realm. Ludwig Mies van der Rohe, the Bauhaus alumnus who went on to design American skyscrapers including New York's Seagram Building, famously said of modern architecture's disdain for ornament, "Less is more." Diana Vreeland, the doyenne of *Vogue* magazine from 1963 to 1971, was fond of saying, "Elegance is refusal." Steve Jobs, however, worked in an industry that says yes to everything. Microsoft Word is loaded with features no normal user will ever see. Macintosh computers work straight out of the box and are the picture of simplicity.

Predictably, Jobs limited his sermons on the art of saying no to internal Apple audiences. On one occasion, though, he accepted an invitation to opine outside the company. Jerry Yang gathered about two hundred of his top-ranking executives at the Sofitel San Francisco Bay hotel in 2007, shortly after he took back the CEO reins at Yahoo! He wanted to discuss his plans for the troubled company. To boost the sagging spirits of his demoralized executives, he brought in a guest speaker, Steve Jobs. Separated by about a decade in age, Yang and Jobs had much in common. Each had been the celebrated co-founder of a game-changing and wildly successful Silicon Valley company. Each had given up leadership of the company in favor of more seasoned executives. Each had seen his company drift and decline. Now Yang was returning as Yahoo!'s CEO, just as Jobs had done at Apple exactly ten years earlier.

After being introduced by Yang, Jobs recounted the dire straits Apple was in when he returned. He reminded the audience that Apple had about ninety days of cash left. He noted that the Microsoft investment had given Apple some cash cushion, and that Jobs had cut and cut Apple until the iMac was ready to be released. "Strategy is figuring out what not to do," he told the group. Back then, he went on, he specifically rejected pleas from his executives to create a personal digital assistant like the PalmPilot, preferring to focus on rejuvenating the Macintosh line. His advice to Yahoo!: "Just pick one thing you can do that's great. We knew it was the Mac."

Jobs then treated Yang and his executives to some Apple-style honesty. "Yahoo! seems interesting," he said. "Yahoo! can be anything you want. Seriously. You have talented people and more money than you could possibly need," he continued. "I can't figure out, though, if you're a content company or a technology company. Just pick one. I know which I'd pick." Said a former Yahoo! executive who was in the room: "It was humiliating. We knew he was right. But we also knew we were incapable of choosing." (Yang didn't last nearly as long as a second-time CEO as Jobs did. He gave up the job again in 2009, and Yahoo! has continued its steady decline—in part because of its inability to choose.)

For its part, Apple has chosen to say no repeatedly. It didn't make a phone for years, often protesting—arguably disingenuously—that it didn't want to be in the phone business. Apple actually started developing the iPad before the iPhone, but it switched gears out of a sense that the timing wasn't right for a tablet. (The iPhone debuted in 2007; the iPad came three years later.) After having struggled to maintain a significant business selling to corporate customers over the years, Apple deemphasized the "enterprise" altogether. Today, Apple has sales teams that service businesses. But even sizeable companies will buy from Apple resellers, who can offer business-oriented customer service.

Sidelining business-to-business sales is a significant omission in a big tech company's strategy. Jobs explained it away by saying that Apple preferred to sell to users, not IT managers. What's more, with the popularity of its mobile devices, Apple has been succeeding in big corporate environments by marketing to employees rather than information systems professionals. As a result, Apple says 92 percent of the *Fortune* 500 is testing or deploying iPads anyway, just as if Apple had crafted a major initiative to sell to them. In effect, employees have dragged their employers into buying the technology the workers want, a phenomenon called the "consumerization" of IT—a trend Apple has led.

Tim Cook used to say that Apple could put its entire product line on a conference room table. That's a result of the winnowing process that occurred in the post-1997 era. Where once there were multiple computers for sale by Apple, the new team sold only four: two desktops and two notebooks. To this day, Apple offers essentially four versions of its iMac: two sizes of screens, two sizes of processors. (To appreciate the tightness of this assortment, compare the current roster of iMacs with the multiple, horribly named all-in-one PCs Hewlett-Packard offers on its website.)

Simplicity is in the DNA of the company, but also in its lean organizational structure. "Apple is not set up to do twenty amazing things a year," said a former executive. "At most it's three projects that can get a ton of attention at the executive level. It is about editing down. The executive team is always looking at picking technologies at just the right time. The minute you're doing a hundred things, you can't possibly do things the Apple way. Most companies don't want to focus on one thing because they could fail. Winnowing ideas from twenty-five to four is horrifyingly scary."

Saying no is a shock to the system for newcomers to Apple. An executive whose company was acquired by Apple described the process of getting used to turning down deals that didn't meet strict financial terms, shunning attention from the news media, and adhering to rigid pricing schedules. "[The power of restraint] probably gets instilled into you as much as anything else, the minimalist approach of not overreaching on deals, not overreaching with PR, not overreaching in your conversations, not overreaching on anything," the executive said.

The art of refusal extends to the products themselves. Internal critics often pointed to Jobs's inability to bless more than a handful of projects with his attention. But avoiding "feature creep" is a hallmark of good product design that's taken seriously at Apple. On the plus side, this is what leads to a music player with one button or a desktop computer that isn't littered with the "crapware"— a favorite Steve Jobs put-down—that other PC makers inflict on their customers. On the downside, the focused mind-set delays the introduction of features that everyone knows customers want and that Apple has every intention of giving them. "How long did it take to get 'cut and paste' into iOS?" asked one frustrated former executive—

an iPhone user, obviously. As a point of fact, it took two years; iPhone 3GS, introduced in June 2009, was the first in which Apple's mobile operating system incorporated the basic computing ability of cutting and pasting text. The first iPad had no camera, giving customers a reason to buy an iPad 2 when it came out a year later.

Perhaps Apple's most radical act of refusal is the way executives at the highest ranks will not chase revenue for revenue's sake. It's not that Apple isn't interested in making money, naturally, nor that it hasn't done a good job at it. The point is that the Apple culture doesn't begin with an exploration of how to make the most money. "Steve's talked about the goal of Apple, and the goal of Apple is not to make money but to make really nice products, really great products," said Jonathan Ive, Apple's design chief, at the Art Center College of Design's Radical Craft conference in 2006. "That is our goal and as a consequence if they are good, people will buy them and we'll make money." Indeed, Apple's behavior is littered with examples of downright revenue avoidance. PC makers put crapware on their computers—antivirus software, subscription offers, and so on—precisely because the revenue is lucrative. Apple forgoes such opportunities time and again, convinced that high-quality products will ultimately generate more profits. It's a classic long-term approach.

Even the way Apple does collect money from its customers reflects its minimalist mind-set. Recognizing that waiting in line is a major downer for customers, and one that slows the sales process, Apple figured out how to empower its "sales specialists" in retail stores to check out customers from the floor. Anything at all to speed up and simplify the experience was a good idea. "We measured how fast could we turn around something at the Genius Bar, because that made people smile," recalled George Blankenship, a former top executive in Apple's retail unit. "How fast can we get people through the register? Well, let's get rid of the register. Why do we even need a register?" (Apple retail employees take credit cards or iTunes account numbers from anywhere on the floor.) In the words of Rob Schoeben, the former product marketing executive: "Apple obsesses over the user experience, not revenue optimization."

4

Stay Start-Up Hungry

When Steve Jobs rejoined Apple in 1997, it looked like big companies everywhere. *Like other companies* is precisely what Jobs did not want Apple to be.

The company had grown bureaucratic under the professional managers who supplanted the co-founder. Apple had factories in the United States and around the world. Multiple committees existed to address various corporate imperatives. Among its managerial ranks, fiefdoms had arisen, each with budgeting power and sometimes-competing agendas. Among the things the Apple of the mid-1990s lacked was a cohesive mission.

From the moment Jobs returned, the corporate culture changed. Now it would move in unison, fiefdoms would be banished, and employees would focus on whatever it was they did best—and nothing else. To this day, graphics runs graphics; logistics controls logistics; finance worries about the bottom line. Today's corporate structure makes for a marked contrast with what Jobs encountered upon his return from NeXT.

Apple's approach to advertising at the time of Jobs's return is indicative of how it had lost the tight focus and the entrepreneurial *oomph* of a start-up. Jobs would tell the story of confronting sixteen divisions at Apple, each with a divisional advertising budget. He put an end to that quickly, declaring that from that point onward, there would be one advertising budget; divisions would compete for ad dollars. Jobs would later brag that Apple's overall ad spending *rose* in short order. Despite the company's difficult financial position, the consolidation was about a renewed commitment to promoting Apple and its products, and not out of any sense of obligation to one division or executive—nor even to save money. The hottest products commandeered the most ad dollars. The focus obviously paid off, and Apple continued the practice of heavily promoting fewer rather than more products. Once things really picked up, a virtuous halo effect took hold: Heavy promotions of iPods brought people into retail stores, where customers were exposed to Macs. iPod advertising indirectly drove the sales of computers—even if Apple wasn't currently pumping huge ad dollars into the category.

The ailing bottom line exposed the need for a healthier corporate structure. Apple was losing money in the mid-1990s despite operating what looked like profitable businesses. An example was its printer division, which according to Apple's accounting at the time delivered a positive "contribution margin" to the company. Apple printers offered nothing differentiated to customers, however, and a more honest accounting of corporate overhead revealed the division to be a dog. Printers were among the products that Jobs summarily killed. (The Newton hand-held computer, famously, was another.)

What emerged over the years, as Apple transformed itself from a fallen idol to a world beater, is an organization that tries as hard as any big company can to embrace the ethos of a start-up. The benefits are not always obvious to those outside 1 Infinite Loop. With a handful of bold steps such as insulating all but a few employees from the profit-and-loss figures as well as using an extreme form of accountability, Apple has created a work environment where employees are encouraged to think big thoughts yet mediocrity becomes quickly exposed.

Jobs often told audiences that there were no commit-tees at Apple. Ex-employees have questioned this asser-tion, pointing to entities that looked and sounded like committees, including an international pricing commit-tee and a brand committee. What they don't dispute is that Jobs fostered a culture that eschewed standing, task-oriented groups that deflected attention from the primary and single-minded goal of executing Apple's plans. "The reason you have committees is that you have divided responsibilities," Jobs said. "We don't. At Apple you can figure out exactly who is responsible."

The notion of responsibility is enshrined at Apple in a company acronym, the DRI. It stands for "Directly Respon-sible Individual," and it is the person on any given assign-ment who will be called on the carpet if something isn't done right. Interestingly, the term *DRI* predates the return of Steve Jobs. For him, responsibility was part of Apple's culture, not a word in an acronym. Employees many rungs down the ladder from the CEO echo the sentiment. "When you talk to people at Apple, they can tell you in general what they do," said a former senior hardware executive. "When you interview people at other companies it is amazing how few of them can say what they do." Reported another departed employee, this one from Apple's marketing ranks: "There's no confusion as to who's going to do what. It's very detail-oriented. I tried to bring this to other places, and they were like, 'What do you mean?' They wanted two to three people to have responsibility."

The DRI is a powerful management tool, enshrined as an Apple corporate best practice, passed on by word of mouth to new generations of employees. "Any effective meeting at Apple will have an action list," said a former employee. "Next to it will be the DRI." Typical is the way Apple's event marketing group prepares a document called "At a Glance," a detailed schedule for the production of events. Each item, along with the time and place it will occur, includes a DRI. Similarly, in the weeks and months leading up to a product debut, the manual known internally as the *Rules of the Road* has DRIs assigned for even the smallest items. "When we'd go through a launch, each task would have a DRI listed," said an ex-employee. "That's the person who's on the hook."

Just as Jobs made *committee* a dirty word at Apple, he also snuffed out that standby of managerial power, the "P&L." In the rest of the corporate world, to say one manages a profit-and-loss statement is to proclaim one's domain. *I run my own P&L, therefore I am.* The executive with a P&L has the authority—and the burden—to make profits for the company. Hiring and firing decisions, strategy, and resource allocation belong to P&L-wielding executives, often those with *general manager* in their titles, in addition to some variant of *vice president*.

Under Steve Jobs, only one executive "owned" a P&L, and that was the chief financial officer. By creating a system whereby only a financial executive would mind the budget, Jobs forced functional executives to focus on their strengths. Managers at all levels of Apple said they rarely were pressed for any kind of financial analysis or to defend decisions based on potential return on investment. Said a former marketing executive: "I can't recall one discussion when the conversation was about dollars or expenses." It's a common refrain when talking to ex–Apple people. The reason they didn't discuss expenses is almost certainly because their bosses didn't, either. Jobs held that authority himself and monitored it solely through his CFO. Apple managers and their employees almost behave like talented rich kids: They have access to unlimited resources to do interesting things. They do not have to think about what ideas, components, and experiences might cost. They are only limited by what their "parents" will give them.

Aside from this removal of profit-and-loss concerns, another way that Apple is at odds with many corporations is in organizing along functional lines rather than by product groups or other structural conceits. Few big companies are able to organize along functional lines. That's why above a certain size, big corporations carve themselves up into divisions. Yet the functional nature of Apple's management is key to its success. When Ron Johnson left Target to lead Apple's retail effort, he was not given control over retail inventory. Tim Cook, then Apple's senior vice president for worldwide operations, held this. Johnson didn't choose which products to put in the stores. He put all Apple products in the stores. Johnson controlled plenty, of course, including site selection, design, real estate acquisition, training, and so forth. In most companies, the executive who runs the commerce website would control the photographic images on the site. Not at Apple, where one graphic arts team chooses images for the entire company.

In this alternative management structure, executives have limited power but also aren't expected to have skills that check some all-star management box. You're hired and appreciated for your ability on the field, not your ability as a coach or manager. Jonathan Ive, widely admired for his design ideas, is considered to have little grasp of finance. This could be seen as a negative: One of the most powerful executives at Apple, one who had the ear of Steve Jobs for years, isn't viewed as having business chops. The upside, however, has served Apple extremely well. Ive is known to make seemingly unrealistic demands on the manufacturing and operations teams in pursuit of his design vision. Paying for his vision is someone else's problem, and Apple's products have been the outcome. Ive's dreamy insistence on a stainless-steel bezel for iPhones and industrial-grade glass for iPads, for instance, paid off in a way that managers worried about making a budget never could have achieved. If he were handcuffed to a spreadsheet, would Ive have insisted that the Italian marble being considered for Apple's first Manhattan retail store be flown to Cupertino for him to inspect?

The very concept of general management—the notion of promoting well-rounded, left-brain/right-brain types who can toggle from real estate to supply chain to marketing to finance—constitutes an organizational third rail at Apple. This approach contradicts about a century of business school teaching in the industrialized world, particularly the general-management concepts taught in the post–World War II era at the Harvard Business School. Befitting his bias toward the vibe of a start-up, Jobs was long disdainful of general management. While building Apple in the 1980s, he denigrated big companies such as Polaroid and Xerox for having lost their way. "Companies, as they grow to become multi-billion-dollar entities, somehow lose their vision," he told *Playboy* in 1985. "They insert lots of layers of middle management between the people running the company and the people doing the work. They no longer have an inherent feel or passion about the products. The creative people, who are the ones who care passionately, have to persuade five layers of management to do what they know is the right thing to do."

When Jobs returned to Apple, he was disgusted to find that it had become one of those companies he had disparaged a decade earlier. "What was wrong with Apple wasn't individual contributors," he said. "We had to get rid of about four thousand middle managers. Good technical people stepped up to become managers." Jobs was well aware that Apple's approach stood apart. "The way you grow at Apple is not the same as at GE," he said. "We don't send you on assignment to the Congo. We don't have this notion that a manager can manage anything."

The Apple approach to management and talent development is top-down. It begins with an all-knowing CEO aided by a powerful executive team—the "ET," as it is known throughout the company. "The purpose of the executive team is to coordinate things and set the tone for the company," Jobs once said. This ten-member group, including the CEO, comprises the heads of product marketing, hardware and software engineering, operations, retail stores, Internet services, and design, all of whom directly have a hand in Apple's products. They're joined by the heads of finance and legal.

The executive team meets each Monday, with the main action items being a review of Apple's product plans. It may seem like a typical corporate function, but it's unusual in the depth of the attention paid to the granular aspects of product development. Because Apple has so few products, the executive team is able to review all of them over the course of two weekly meetings. The company may be top-down, but the executive-team format engenders a system of managing up. Teams throughout the company are in a constant state of preparing their boss or their boss's boss to present at an executive-team meeting. Indeed, individual groups throughout the company have their own meetings to prepare for the ET and other top-level meetings. (When he ran operations, Tim Cook convened his pre-ET meeting by telephone on Sunday nights.) "Everybody is working toward these Monday presentations," said Andrew Borovsky, a former Apple designer. "There is executive review of every significant project."

Adherence to this communicate-up/manage-down system explains Apple's speed and clarity of decision making. "You're never out of a two-week decision loop," said one former hardware executive. (Jobs said that if a product discussion wasn't finished one week, it would be added to the following week's agenda.) "Young engineers know their work gets presented. They know their work matters."

They also know debate will not be endless. "Someone once said to me, 'I didn't always agree, but I knew there was going to be a decision,'" noted this same engineer.

The weekly top-level product review also serves as a kind of graduate seminar for executives below the level of the executive team. As executives added more responsibility, Jobs would invite them to attend portions of the ET meetings, then more and then more still.

The speediness of Apple's decision making also is aided by how judiciously information is communicated outside the executive team. Typically, more information goes in than goes out. Apple teams are given swift feedback—but only the feedback they are deemed to need. The need-to-know mentality explains all the cordoned-off secret rooms with restrictive badge access. By selectively keeping some employees from concerning themselves with colleagues elsewhere in a giant company, Apple creates the illusion that these employees in fact don't work for a giant company. They work for a start-up. "Some of it is theater, some of it is paranoia," said a former Apple engineer. But it's also done with a purpose. "They are isolating themselves from everything that is bad about a big company."

The original iPhone team, for example, didn't interact with the people working on the iPod, then the dominant and fastest-growing product at Apple. The iPhone organization was allowed to raid the iPod group and other areas of the company for engineering talent. That's because the iPhone was a corporate priority, driven from the top. "A big company would have worried about cannibalizing the iPod," said an observer who knew executives in both groups. "There would have been cultural and technical tension." Effects of any tension were minimized at Apple because the two groups didn't talk. The start-up team could pretend it didn't have the baggage of a big corporation.

Put these corporate attributes together—clear direction, individual accountability, a sense of urgency, constant feedback, clarity of mission—and you begin to have a sense of Apple's values. *Values* may be a squishy topic in the corporate world, a term that's interchangeable with *culture* or *core beliefs*. In the case of Apple, however, being able to assess how deeply ingrained its values are informs the question of how the company will fare without Steve Jobs. After all, Jobs himself agonized over the drift in Apple's values during the ten-plus years he was in the wilderness at NeXT and Pixar. "What ruined Apple wasn't growth," he said in a 1995 interview with the Smithsonian Institution, as he watched his beloved brainchild flailing. "What ruined Apple was values. John Sculley ruined Apple and he ruined it by bringing a set of values to the top of Apple which were corrupt and corrupted some of the top people who were there, drove out some of the ones who were not corruptible, and brought in more corrupt ones and paid themselves collectively tens of millions of dollars and cared more about their own glory and wealth than they did about what built Apple in the first place, which was making great computers for people to use." (In 2011, Sculley first declined to comment on Jobs's decade-old comments, and then followed up to cite his accomplishments at Apple, including helping to usher in the Macintosh. It's worth noting that *corrupt* was a favorite pejorative for Jobs. He generally used it to describe his opinion of the wrong way of doing things, as opposed to implying illegal wrongdoing.)

If Jobs thought the leadership during the interregnum obsessed about money, the modern obsession with user experience has created a kind of shorthand for how Apple employees communicate. "There's a passion about the place," said a former top engineering executive. "You interact with people at other companies who just aren't connected. They are floating above the strategy. You try explaining to them what not to do, and it's like talking to people in a language they don't understand. At Apple, thirteen of fifteen topics get cut off after a sentence of discussion. That's all that's needed."

The Apple way is direct and deadline-oriented. "Dates are set well in advance," said Mike Janes, who ran Apple's online store in the early 2000s. "Things get accomplished. There are no questions. The 'Innovator's Dilemma' doesn't exist at Apple," he said, referring to Clay Christensen's popular book about how big companies fail to anticipate the next wave because they are unwilling to sacrifice existing sales. "There's no dilemma." As for urgency, "If you want to get something done, the meeting is this afternoon. Or tomorrow. You don't wait to get something on the calendar."

For such a sprawling organization, Apple also is a headquarters-centric company. Sure, there are sales offices and retail stores throughout the world. And Apple has established China as its base of manufacturing. But its entire management team is based in Cupertino and talks to one another, frequently and in person. The small number of vice presidents, typically reporting directly to members of the executive team, means that the CEO can see the entire company with one degree of separation. Apple people board airplanes at the drop of a hat, but the company does not have a videoconferencing or conference-call culture. Meetings generally happen in Cupertino.

Moreover, there's a sense that only people in Cupertino are truly to be trusted. Bob Borchers, the former iPhone product marketing executive, recalled the decision to fly more than forty people from headquarters to Europe for the iPhone launch in the United Kingdom and Germany. "It was Cupertino staff, the folks who'd been part of the launch at Macworld, who had already been through it," he said, referring to the iPhone's debut in 2007 at the Moscone Center in San Francisco. "So rather than trying to train somebody, even somebody in the regional office, we said, 'No, let's take the people who have done this before. Let's fly them over.' We essentially shut down all of product marketing for a week."

In a company organized along functional rather than divisional lines, scouting must be a core competency of its leader. Steve Jobs long considered the issue of spotting and grooming talent to be one of the most important aspects of being an entrepreneur and a CEO. It was particularly on his mind in 1995, a decade after being pushed aside at Apple and two years before his return. Listen to how, in the Smithsonian interview, he discussed the relative numerical value of people in the way a hedge-fund manager might discuss leverage.

I always considered part of my job was to keep the quality level of people in the organizations I work with very high. That's what I consider one of the few things I actually can contribute individually—to really try to instill in the organization the goal of only having "A" players. Because in this field, like in a lot of fields, the difference between the worst taxicab driver and the best taxicab driver to get you cross-town Manhattan might be two to one. The best one will get you there in fifteen minutes, the worst one will get you there in a half an hour. Or the best cook and the worst cook, maybe it's three to one. Pick something like that. In the field that I'm in the difference between the best person and the worst person is about a hundred to one or more. The difference between a good software person and a great software person is fifty to one, twenty-five to fifty to one, huge dynamic range. Therefore, I have found, not just in software, but in everything I've done it really pays to go after the best people in the world.

Mike Janes, a former Apple executive, remembered a more concise Steve-ism on the subject of talent: "A players hire A players, and B players hire C players. We want only A players here."

Once hired, people stay at Apple for years, assuming they have learned to accept the literal and the unspoken terms of employment. At the time Steve Jobs resigned as CEO, every member of the executive team except for the general counsel and chief financial officer had been in their jobs since at least 2000. The same was true in the middle ranks, especially among engineers, who'd dreamed of working at Apple since they were old enough to buy their first Mac. Rival recruiters say it is difficult to hire people out of Apple, particularly engineers. Successful employees do leave, of course. Asked why, a typical cup-half-full response revolves around a desire to pursue one's own dreams instead of Apple's. "At Apple you work on Apple products," said former Apple designer Borovsky. He left to start his own design consultancy.

Apple people undoubtedly are world-class, but being excellent at your job is not enough. It takes a certain kind of egoless and fanatical person to thrive at Apple. First, Apple employees, whether extremely senior or entry-level, must have the ability to "check their identities at the door," in the words of one former executive. "At Apple you are hired for a specialty, and it's good for the company." Jobs once bragged about having the best metallurgists in the world at Apple. On the flip side, there is little movement internally, and more recently a bias toward hiring from the outside has become apparent, what one recruiter calls "a replacement culture versus a development culture." Said an executive who worked at Apple twice: "I have way more examples of people being demoted than promoted. They'd be banished from one group, left to find a lesser position elsewhere in Apple and continue [waiting for their stock options to] vest." The frequent quip from an Apple employee who accepts demotion calls to mind how you refer to the last-ranked graduate of medical school (a doctor): "I still work at Apple."

Apple is not for everyone. "Apple runs so fast and so lean, it requires people to really work hard and take on a lot of tasks and do them in a short period of time," said a recruiter who is close to Apple employees. "There's a mystique about Apple that is intriguing to people, so they want to check it out. They want to be part of something cool, but then they get in there and they're like, *Oh, this really isn't the hip company that I thought it was.*" In fact, there's a popular expression at Apple: Everybody at Apple wants out, and everybody outside Apple wants in.

There are downsides to the Apple way. Charles O'Reilly, a professor at Stanford's Graduate School of Business who studies leadership, organizational culture, and demography, believes there's only one reason Apple has been able to stave off a traditional organizational structure in favor of a functional one. "Apple has been able to avoid being a big, market-driven organization because Jobs made all the decisions," he said. "We tend to worship at the altar of success," he added, guessing that without Jobs the lack of general management will change from an oddity to a liability. Indeed, around the time Jobs stepped down, Apple was conducting multiple searches for top-level executives, including a new head of retail, a number two for product marketing, and a new sales chief, because sales had reported to Cook. Apple's organization chart is so tight—approximately seventy VPs for a company with just over twenty-four thousand non-retail employees—that its bench is relatively shallow.

The ability to maintain a low profile is often hard for the go-getter overachievers whom Apple recruits. For years, the only executive Jobs allowed to serve on an outside board of directors was Tim Cook, who is on the board of Nike. Other employees have been warned not to attach their names to the causes of nonprofit organizations, at least not in a way that would identify them as employees of Apple. Clearly the company didn't want individual employees "speaking" for Apple. Jobs suggested his biggest concern was one of distraction. Andy Miller, who joined Apple as a vice president after Apple bought his mobile advertising company in 2009, asked Jobs if he could join the board of an independent company in a different business than Apple. "What?" Jobs responded. "You're barely cutting it here," Jobs said, which Miller understood to be relatively high praise, "and you want to go spend your time helping someone else's company? I don't even let Forstall out of the office," Jobs added, referring to Scott Forstall, Apple's mobile software chief, a high-ranking and considerably more influential executive than Miller. Needless to say, Miller declined the board membership offer.

Lack of extracurricular activities breeds focus, but it also fosters insularity. Macintosh-era Apple executives in particular may have gone their entire tenures at Apple without meaningfully interacting with outsiders other than a handful of close suppliers. After all, they built their careers before iTunes and the iPhone thrust Apple into so many new industry conversations. "I fundamentally believe that people who stay too long can't work anywhere else," said one executive who has gone to work elsewhere. "It doesn't translate into real life." Another departed executive likened a recently retired colleague to a newly freed convict. "It's as if he'd been in jail for two decades when he got out. He knows no one."

Typical Apple employees, in fact, don't need to know many people at all—just a handful of colleagues in their immediate group. The anthropologist Robin Dunbar theorized in 1992 that humans are capable of maintaining meaningful relationships with no more than an average of 150 people simultaneously. He came to this conclusion after scientifically observing primates in the wild and their "self-grooming" habits—in other words, the way they nurtured and supported one another in the pursuit of life-sustaining tasks. Steve Jobs observed a different group of creatures—engineers working on the first Macintosh computer in the 1980s—and came to a similar conclusion. He declared during his first tour at Apple that he never wanted the Macintosh division to be larger than one hundred people.

Small group sizes, and the number one hundred in particular, have been integral to the Apple culture ever since. Apple isn't alone in this. Companies are forever trying to figure out how to foster separate "skunk works" projects or commit discrete SWAT teams to important assignments. Amazon.com had a "two-pizza" rule: Teams couldn't be bigger than the number of people that could be fed by two pizzas in the (likely) event they were working late and got the munchies.

Apple frequently assigns major projects to small groups. For example, just two engineers wrote the code for converting Apple's Safari browser for the iPad, a massive undertaking. It is, after all, how a start-up would approach something important, though in the start-up's case it would be because there aren't a lot of people around—a necessity rather than a conscious management decision. "If two to four people can get it done, you don't need twenty to thirty, which is how so many other companies do it," said Andrew Borovsky, the former Apple designer. "At Apple, really small teams work on really important projects. That is one of the advantages of being in a start-up."

Jobs enshrined the importance of a small group in an ultra-secret gathering called the "Top 100." The expression refers to both the group and the meeting, which was held more or less annually when Jobs was well and less consistently when he wasn't. Jobs described the group alternatively as those he would choose if he were to start the company over again and the people he'd want with him in the proverbial life raft should the good ship Apple sink. Attendance at a Top 100 was a highly coveted and emotionally charged moment in an executive's career because Jobs doled out invites based on his opinion of the individuals in question rather than their rank. Relatively low-level engineers would attend, because Jobs wanted them there, while certain vice presidents would be excluded. Hurt feelings over exclusion were the norm, which is what Jobs expected and even relished.

Everything about the Top 100 was shrouded in secrecy. For years it was held at the Chaminade Resort & Spa in Santa Cruz, California, and later at the Carmel Valley Ranch, on the opposite side of the Monterey Bay. Attendees were prohibited from driving themselves to the meeting. Instead these essential and wealthy executives boarded a bus in Cupertino for the drive south. Participants were told not to put the meeting on their calendars and not to discuss it internally. That was folly, of course, because senior executives needed help from their subordinates to get ready for their roles in the meeting. "We would prepare materials for people who would attend the Top 100," remembered Michael Hailey, a manager who was not among the elect to be invited. "Then we'd tongue-in-cheek have a Bottom 100 lunch after they were gone."

So secretive were the details of the Top 100 meeting

that Apple had the meeting rooms swept for bugs beforehand. Jobs was known to forbid food servers from entering the room while products were being shown. He once encouraged attendees to introduce themselves to the person sitting next to them to ensure that no one had snuck into the room.

Once ensconced at their exclusive off-site, the Top 100 were treated to a thorough review of Apple's product plans for the next eighteen months or so. Jobs sat at the front of the room, kicking things off with a presentation that described his vision for the company and then presiding over presentations by other executives. Executives who attended said the presentations were of the caliber of a Steve Jobs keynote, meaning that tremendous effort went into them. "There would be half a dozen presentations a day, each only an hour long," recalled an executive who attended many Top 100s. "You could really talk about anything in those meetings. You didn't have to worry about secrecy. You could put everything out on the table: the pros, the cons, all that kind of stuff."

The meetings were intended to allow the level of leadership below the executive team—people who in such a siloed and segregated company wouldn't ordinarily interact with one another—to bond. They were also a venue for sneak peeks at upcoming products. The store concept was revealed at a Top 100. So was the first iPod.

At the last Top 100 Steve Jobs attended, in November 2010, he showed off the iPad 2 and its colorful new magnetic cover—four months before the public got to see it. A highlight for attendees was an extended Q&A between Jobs and his executives. One asked why Jobs himself wasn't more philanthropic. He responded that he thought giving away money was a waste of time. The San Francisco Giants won the World Series during a dinner session of that last Top 100—a distraction to the many Giants fans in the room, and an irritant to Jobs, who was completely uninterested in sports.

The Top 100 was a mostly internal affair, though the rare external guest made an appearance. Intel chief executive Paul Otellini presented the year Apple and Intel began a partnership to place Intel chips in Macs. As Apple prepared to enter the phone business, its key contacts at AT&T, Glenn Lurie and Paul Roth, briefed the computer-industry executives on the wireless world and its history. Lurie remembered the meeting for having exposed him to Apple executives beyond the narrow group with whom he'd been dealing on the iPhone. "I walked away incredibly impressed with the individuals," he said. (Lurie's role with Apple is so important to him that his official AT&T bio states that he has "responsibilities for AT&T's ongoing operations and relationship with Apple Inc., having led negotiations to bring the iPhone to AT&T." It notes his brief career as a professional soccer player but doesn't mention the name of any other AT&T partner.)

Those left behind described excessive whispering and neck craning over empty offices and the absence of VIPs during the meeting, which didn't officially exist on anyone's agenda. "We weren't supposed to know where they were. But we all knew where they were," recalled someone who had not made it into Steve Jobs's life raft. "They in turn weren't supposed to be working while they were there, but they'd do emails and take phone breaks to avoid falling too far behind."

While versions of the Top 100 exist at other companies, these off-sites are usually more egalitarian in the guest list and contain some training component that suggests to attendees they are being considered to move up the organizational chart. Apple's approach to career development is yet another way it runs contrary to the norms at other companies. The prevalent attitude for workers in the corporate world is to consider their growth trajectory. *What's my path up? How can I get to the next level?* Companies, in turn, spend an inordinate amount of time and money grooming their people for new responsibilities. They labor to find just the right place for people. But what if it turns out that all that thinking is wrong? What if companies encouraged employees to be satisfied where they are, because they're good at what they do, not to mention because that might be what's best for shareholders?

Instead of employees fretting that they were stuck in terminal jobs, what if they exalted in having found their *perfect* jobs? A certain amount of office politics might evaporate in a corporate culture where career growth is not considered tantamount to professional fulfillment. Shareholders, after all, don't care about fiefdoms and egos. There are many professionals who would find it liberating to work at what they are good at, receive competitive killer compensation, and not have to worry about supervising others or jockeying for higher rungs on an org chart. If more companies did these things, it might work, and it might not. It might not even work so well at Apple after Steve Jobs hasn't been CEO for a few years. But if more companies thought about such things, they'd most certainly be more like Apple.

5

Hire Disciples

On January 21, 2009, exactly a week after Steve Jobs announced a six-month medical leave of absence, Tim Cook presided over a conference call with Wall Street analysts and investors following the release of Apple's quarterly earnings. Predictably, the very first questioner wanted to know how Cook would run the company differently from Jobs. The analyst also asked the awkward question on everyone's mind: Would Cook succeed Jobs if the CEO didn't return?

Cook didn't brush off the question with the usual bromides that baseball players and executives are so fond of. "There is extraordinary breadth and depth and tenure among the Apple executive team," he began, "and they lead 35,000 employees that I would call wicked smart. And that's in all areas of the company, from engineering to marketing to operations and sales and all the rest. And the values of our company are extremely well entrenched."

Cook certainly could have stopped there. But his emotions were raw at the time, in part because he was genuinely concerned about Jobs's health. He knew the "Apple community"—customers, developers, employees—was concerned, too. So he continued, as if reciting a creed he had learned as a child in Sunday school:

> We believe that we are on the face of the earth to make great products, and that's not changing. We are constantly focusing on innovating.
>
> We believe in the simple not the complex.
>
> We believe that we need to own and control the primary technologies behind the products that we make, and participate only in markets where we can make a significant contribution. We believe in saying no to thousands of projects, so that we can really focus on the few that are truly important and meaningful to us.
>
> We believe in deep collaboration and cross-pollination of our groups, which allow us to innovate in a way that others cannot. And frankly, we don't settle for anything less than excellence in every group in the company, and we have the self-honesty to admit when we're wrong and the courage to change.
>
> And I think regardless of who is in what job those values are so embedded in this company that Apple will do extremely well. And...I strongly believe that Apple is doing the best work in its history.

The apparently extemporaneous statement was extraordinary on a number of levels. For starters, Cook was emphatically hitting all the notes of an oft-played Steve Jobs symphony. He evoked Apple's values. He cited Apple's messianic mission. He ticked off the boxes of simplicity, focus, and relentlessness, all Jobs hallmarks.

More than that, Cook was introducing himself to a slice of the public that barely knew him. True, Cook had been at Apple for more than a decade and had run the company when Jobs first was treated for pancreatic cancer in 2004. Yet he remained a cipher to almost everyone other than a handful of top Apple executives and some of the company's important suppliers and business partners. The basic rap on Cook was that he was the drab automaton who ran all the unglamorous parts of the business Jobs abhorred: supply-chain logistics, product fulfillment, customer support, inventory management, channel sales, hardware manufacturing. And even if he did run the company in Jobs's absence, many believed he'd never be CEO. Right before Jobs stepped down for his 2009 medical leave, a prominent Silicon Valley investor who was unwilling to be quoted by name called the likelihood that Cook would become CEO "laughable," adding that "they don't need a guy who merely gets stuff done. They need a brilliant product guy, and Tim is not that guy. He is an ops guy—at a company where ops is outsourced."

What the investing public, at least, learned from Cook during that earnings call was that there was something of a spark to this fellow, and more than a little ambition. He also revealed himself to be just a bit poetic—or at least someone who can parrot back the poetry learned during time spent inside a prestigious organization. His *We believes* turned out to have been at least a subconscious echo of the "Auburn Creed," an earnest statement of *I believes* recited at Auburn University, Cook's alma mater in his native Alabama:

> I believe that this is a practical world and that I can count only on what I earn. Therefore, I believe in work, hard work.
>
> I believe in education, which gives me the knowledge to work wisely and trains my mind and my hands to work skillfully.
>
> I believe in honesty and truthfulness, without which I cannot win the respect and confidence of my fellow men.
>
> I believe in a sound mind, in a sound body and a spirit that is not afraid, and in clean sports that develop these qualities.
>
> I believe in obedience to law because it protects the rights of all.
>
> I believe in the human touch, which cultivates sympathy with my fellow men and mutual helpfulness and brings happiness for all.
>
> I believe in my Country, because it is a land of freedom and because it is my own home, and that I can best serve that country by "doing justly, loving mercy, and walking humbly with my God."
>
> And because Auburn men and women believe in these things, I believe in Auburn and love it.

Unbeknownst to his listeners, Cook had simultaneously just offered his own version of the "Apple Creed," a wordier version of the long-ago promise by Jobs that Apple would make "insanely great" products. He also cheekily answered the critics who believed that Apple would crumble when Jobs stepped down. (In his authorized biography of Steve Jobs, released just after Jobs's death, Walter Isaacson reported that Jobs was "rankled and deeply depressed" by Cook's comment that "regardless of who is in what job" Apple would continue to do well.) Mr. Back Office just might have more of the Vision Thing than folks had given him credit for.

Cook and each of Jobs's other key lieutenants embody different elements of what it takes to survive and thrive in the Apple ecosystem. Jobs was smart in surrounding himself with a crew who could function as extensions of himself yet had their own superpowers. He did not hire CEOs-in-training. He let people's talent define their jobs, not the jobs define the people. Cook was a ruthless systems guy but one who grew to understand that logistics had to serve some higher mission. Jonathan Ive was a talented designer who long before he came to Apple obsessed over making technology beautiful. Since he had no designs on running the company, he enjoyed some of the greatest freedom of any Apple employee. Scott Forstall, an empathic engineer who could channel Jobs, was able to keep his ambition in check long enough to gain control of the two hottest product groups—iPhones and iPads. Whether Forstall will happily remain a supporting player will be one of the great internal dramas of Cook's tenure.

To succeed in a company where there is obsessive focus on detail and paranoid guarding of secrets, and where employees are asked to work in a state of permanent start-up, you must be willing to mesh your personal ambitions with those of the corporation. You have to forgo your desire to be acknowledged by the outside world and instead derive satisfaction from being a cell in an organism that is changing the world. It is not for everyone. Like the officer candidate who can't endure the abuse of the drill sergeant, some don't make it. Even Apple's board of directors—made up of voluble heavyweights, including former vice president Al Gore, former Genentech CEO Art Levinson, and J.Crew CEO Millard "Mickey" Drexler—toe the line when it comes to Apple. All played a supporting role to Jobs.

If the business consultant Michael Maccoby's description of a "productive narcissist" perfectly captures the personality of an ascendant Steve Jobs and his profound impact on Apple, his analysis also sheds considerable light on the rise of Tim Cook. Maccoby writes:

> Many narcissists can develop a close relationship with one person, a sidekick who acts as an anchor, keeping the narcissistic partner grounded. However, given that narcissistic leaders trust only their own insights and view of reality, the sidekick has to understand the narcissistic leader and what he is trying to achieve. The narcissist must feel that this person, or in some cases persons, is practically an extension of himself. The sidekick must also be sensitive enough to manage the relationship.

Business history is full of such sidekicks. Frank Wells famously played second banana to Michael Eisner at Disney, so much so that Disney-watchers trace Eisner's

decline in the job to Wells's untimely death in a 1994 heli-
copter crash. Donald Keough played the same role to the
legendary Roberto Goizueta at Coca-Cola. Sheryl Sandberg, a former top Google executive and Treasury Department chief of staff for Larry Summers, has made herself
indispensable to Facebook CEO Mark Zuckerberg by running all the aspects of the company that don't interest the
young founder—while not challenging her boss on the
areas that do.

For his part, Timothy Donald Cook, who is fifty-one,
played the trusted aide to Steve Jobs for nearly fifteen
years. He was the perfect casting for Apple's long-running
buddy movie. Where Jobs was mercurial, Cook was calm.
When Jobs cajoled, Cook implored. Jobs eviscerated volu-
bly; Cook did so with so little emotion that one observer
likened the experience to a dressing-down by a seethingly
quiet parent: "You wished he'd scream instead and just get
it over with." Jobs was larger than life; Cook faded into
the woodwork. Jobs was the epitome of right-brain vision,
Cook the embodiment of left-brain efficiency. Jobs bore
the exotic Middle Eastern hues of his biological father and
a kinetic aura that excited those around him. Cook is the
prototypical Southerner: square-jawed, broad-shouldered,
pale-skinned, with graying hair and an overall blandness
to his appearance and demeanor. Jobs wore distinctive
round spectacles. Cook wears barely noticeable clear, rim-
less glasses.

Critically, Cook wasn't threatening to Jobs, there being
no question who was the rock star and who was the
bloke on bass guitar. Jobs's ego could tolerate Cook's rise
because Cook's ego was impossible to discern.

Yet while Apple's visionary was busy changing the

world, its taskmaster quietly was accumulating a tremendous amount of power inside Apple. Cook grabbed
responsibility after responsibility so gradually that almost
until he became CEO no one seemed to notice. An Apple
outsider—worse, he was a longtime PC man who bled
IBM blue—Cook was the last member to join Jobs's
post-1997 executive team. He had grown up in Roberts-
dale, Alabama, a small town "on the way to the beach"
in southern Alabama, and attended Auburn, where he
studied industrial engineering. After college he took a job
at IBM, where he stayed sixteen years, working in the
division in Research Triangle Park, North Carolina, that
manufactured PCs. While at IBM, he picked up a night
school MBA at Duke. In 1997, after a stint as the operations chief of a computer distributor, Cook took a logistics
job at Compaq, then a hot PC maker with an expertise in
just-in-time manufacturing methods.

He didn't last long at Compaq, though, because shortly
after he started Steve Jobs came calling. Jobs recognized
that Apple's manufacturing was a shambles. It owned factories and warehouses spread out around the world, from
Sacramento, California, to Cork, Ireland. By 1998, when
Cook joined Apple, the company was in the process of
pruning everything—from its product roster to its executive ranks. Jobs knew enough about operations to know
that first, Apple's were badly broken, and second, overseeing their repair didn't interest him.

In Cook, Jobs found someone with whom he had
little in common other than musical tastes: They shared
a fondness for the rock-and-roll greats of the 1960s. Yet
he knew Cook could help him slim down the company.

The new recruit quickly closed all of Apple's factories, opting instead to mimic industry leader Dell by outsourcing manufacturing. The goal was to strengthen Apple's balance sheet by cutting down on the wasteful practice of carrying on its books more parts than were needed. Inventory, Cook would later explain, "is fundamentally evil. You want to manage it like you're in the dairy business: If it gets past its freshness date, you have a problem."

Cook quickly developed a fearsome reputation at Apple as a Mr. Fix-it who blended in but didn't take no for an answer. Recalled a senior colleague from that era: "Tim Cook is the kind of guy who just doesn't get flustered." His meetings were legendary for their length and the breadth of detail he'd require from his staff, many of whom he recruited from IBM. Cook's palette was a spreadsheet, and he'd study each line before meetings with his vice presidents. "They're nervous going into that meeting," said an employee who knew Cook's group. "He'll say, 'What's this variance on column D, line 514? What's the root cause of that?' And if someone doesn't know the details, they get flayed right there in the meeting." Unlike Jobs, though, Cook was even-keeled. "I don't recall his once raising his voice," said Mike Janes, who worked for Cook. "His ability to go from forty thousand feet to nose-against-the-windshield is amazing."

Like Jobs, Cook accepted no excuses. Early in his tenure, Cook remarked at a meeting with his team that a certain situation in Asia was a real problem and that one of his executives ought to be in China dealing with it. The meeting continued for another half hour or so, when Cook stopped abruptly, looked up at one of his executives, and asked in all seriousness: "Why are you still here?" The executive stood up, drove to the airport without a change of clothes, and flew to China.

Cook was known for his prodigious memory and command of the facts. "The man can process an insane amount of data and know it down to the technical level," said Steve Doil, who also worked for Cook. "Other CEOs and COOs will tell you 'I have people who can tell you that.' Not Tim. He knows. He can walk around campus and know in great detail enough to ask something like: 'How are iPod repairs going in China?'"

Over time, Cook picked up one after another of the responsibilities from the original members of the Apple management team, consolidating his authority over every operational aspect of the company that wasn't considered "creative."

First he took over sales, which before Apple opened its retail locations primarily meant selling through retailers and other resellers. Next he took on customer support and later Macintosh hardware, already a maturing business by the time the iPod surged in popularity. When the iPhone came out, Cook spearheaded negotiations with wireless carriers around the world.

He had his first taste of running the company when he filled in for two months in 2004 after Jobs had surgery to remove a cancerous tumor from his pancreas. He again covered for Jobs during the six months in 2009 when he received a liver transplant, and again in early 2011, when Jobs stepped aside for his final medical leave. It was a popular parlor game in Silicon Valley during 2011 to wonder if Cook would succeed Jobs, but insiders knew he already was running the company—even as Jobs continued to weigh in on important decisions and to nurture major initiatives. Six weeks before Steve Jobs died, Apple's board of directors named Cook CEO as well as a member of the board.

It is no coincidence that the more responsibility Cook took on in the nuts-and-bolts parts of Apple, the more Jobs was freed up for his creative endeavors. Released from worrying whether customer service was operating smoothly or if retail outlets were receiving inventory to match customer demand, Jobs spent the last decade of his life dreaming up the iPod, iPhone, and iPad—and then marketing them. Jobs could make his impossible demands—longer battery life, flash memory where a disk drive had been—and move on to the next task while his orders were being implemented.

Though not a product designer or a marketer himself, Cook fit in culturally at Apple. In an organization that frowned on talking about money, Cook was extraordinarily frugal. Well after he had sold more than $100 million in Apple stock, he rented a modest home in Palo Alto, a little over a mile from where Jobs lived. (In 2010, Cook finally bought a house of his own, not far from his previous rental, but hardly an extravagant one. Public records indicate he purchased the house for $1.9 million, which in Palo Alto qualifies as a modest abode.) Asked why he lived so humbly, he once said: "I like to be reminded of where I came from, and putting myself in modest surroundings helps me do that. Money is not a motivator for me." (Motivation or not, upon elevating him to CEO, Apple's board awarded Cook a million shares of restricted stock, half of which vest in five years and the balance in ten. Assuming Cook stays the full decade, the grant was worth $400 million at the time the shares were issued.)

In a company chock-full of workaholics, Cook stood out for his all-work-no-play reputation. Single and, as far as any of his colleagues knew, unattached, his idea of a fun vacation was hiking in Yosemite National Park. Cook cycled for recreation and often turned up at an upscale Palo Alto fitness club for 5:30 a.m. workouts. Asked at Apple's 2011 annual shareholder meeting if he had seen a one-man play in Berkeley, California, that depicted Apple's outsourcing practices in an unfavorable light, Cook replied: "Unfortunately if it's not on ESPN or CNBC I don't see it."

Cook took naturally to the requirement that anyone working for Steve Jobs needed to have a low profile. He gave money to Auburn, where alumni association officials noted his lack of a need for recognition. But Cook was allowed to take certain steps that showed he was being groomed for a bigger role. Apple executives generally are prohibited from non-Apple assignments, but Cook joined the board of Nike, seen as a broadening experience for him as well as an opportunity to observe another iconic founder, Phil Knight. Even at Nike, Cook remained low-key. "He never discusses Apple personalities or his accomplishments at Apple," said John Connors, a fellow board member and onetime chief financial officer of Microsoft. "He's the General Petraeus of the corporate world, the kind of guy who lets his results speak for themselves."

Logistics is in fact a key aspect of military planning, and Cook is responsible for Apple's operational excellence. For example, when Apple knew it would move away from disk drives in its iPods and MacBook Air notebooks, it invested in billion-dollar forward purchases of flash memory. Cook's supply-chain organization executed this masterstroke, which accomplished the trifecta of securing Apple's supply, locking in the lowest price, and hobbling the competition's access to components. Such back-of-the-shop excellence at a company known for its creative flair is a rare example of what researchers Charles O'Reilly of Stanford and Michael Tushman, a professor of organizational behavior at the Harvard Business School, refer to as "ambidexterity as a dynamic capability." In other words, it reflects the ability of a top-performing company to be simultaneously efficient and innovative. As noted, Cook's efficiency is what freed up Steve Jobs to be so innovative. After all, the two ways a company makes money are by growing revenues and cutting costs. Apple does both, and the operations machinery that Cook built is the engine that drives down costs while enabling the products that lead to growth.

The obvious question about Cook, though, is whether he has the personality to lead an organization created in the image of Steve Jobs. In public, Cook has a winning smile and a dry wit. Back when Apple had to try harder to convince PC users to buy Macs, it added the capability to run Windows on a Mac. Demonstrating the function at a Mac event, Cook displayed the hated Microsoft's software and deadpanned: "It sends shivers up my spine, but the fact is it's working." He once told a group of investors that "the iPhone was just below food and water on Maslow's hierarchy of needs," according to Sanford Bernstein research analyst Toni Sacconaghi, who witnessed the quip.

Still, in the manner that Maccoby categorizes business

executives, Cook is a classic obsessive, someone who ensures that things get done rather than providing a vision of how things should be. He so thoroughly avoided the spotlight while Jobs was alive that it's almost a given he will share it, as he indeed did at his first public event after becoming CEO, the launch of the iPhone 4S. This is certain to endear Cook to his executives. His fans insist he can in fact inspire as well as direct. "If you believe that charisma is authenticity, he has it," said John Thompson, vice chairman of the search firm Heidrick & Struggles, which recruited Cook to Apple. "He doesn't overstate. But he doesn't understate, either. When you listen to him, you think, *It's highly likely this guy is telling the truth.*"

When he was healthy, Steve Jobs would often be seen in the Apple cafeteria at lunchtime dining alone with Jonathan Ive. Called "Jony" by friends, colleagues, and design geeks, Ive, who is forty-four, is the one personality at Apple other than himself that Jobs tolerated having a public profile. (Presumably Jobs put up with Ive's public renown out of genuine affection as well as a desire to keep Ive happy.)

Ive once starred in an Apple video on manufacturing the aluminum uniframe body for the MacBook Air. He speaks at the occasional design conference. He lends his name to designs of famous Apple products on display at the Museum of Modern Art in New York and the Pompidou museum in Paris. In 2006, Queen Elizabeth II made him a Commander of the British Empire, one step below knighthood.

Though many assume Jobs somehow created Ive, the designer predated Jobs's return to Apple. A graduate of

Newcastle Polytechnic (now Northumbria University) in the UK, he and a business partner founded Tangerine, a design shop whose projects for clients included combs, power tools, and, just before he left, a toilet. Tangerine did some work on nascent laptops for Apple, which landed Ive a job in California in 1992 and a promotion to the head of industrial design four years later, all while Jobs was still in exile. Jobs took an immediate liking to Ive upon his return in 1997 after seeing the prototypes Ive had built in his work area. Shortly afterward Ive led the design for the iMac, the brightly colored computer-in-a-translucent-monitor that saved the company.

Ive meanwhile proceeded to assemble a tight-knit and loyal team of about twenty designers, size and longevity being among the key attributes of the group. "I'm part of a very small team, and we've been together for a very long time," Ive said in a 2006 interview at the Radical Craft design conference. "One of the things about that is that there is a very particular energy and a very special sort of momentum you enjoy when you learn stuff as a small group." Many of his industrial-design colleagues hail from Britain and elsewhere outside the United States. In fact, the industrial design team, along with other creative design units, has its own globe-trotting recruiter, Cheline Jaidar, whose appearances at far-flung design schools are treated like royal visits. Ive himself has a fondness for Japan, where he has gone to observe how samurai swords are crafted. For a while he wanted to hire a painting engineer from a Japanese automaker to improve the coatings on Apple's devices.

Ive's friends use words like *sweet* and *nice* and *humble* to describe him—all words rarely attached to Ive's mentor, Steve Jobs. His sweetness doesn't make Ive any less circumspect about talking about Apple, though. (His assistant, in a posting on the professional profile site LinkedIn, listed two characteristics of his service to Ive: first, "Manage Mr. Ive's calendar, correspondence, security, gifts, events, travel, home, office, and approvals"; and second, "Exercise utmost discretion.") But his celebrity in the design world gives him license to wax poetic about Apple's design, if not the inner workings of the company. "We love taking things to pieces and understanding how things are made," he said in the 2006 design conference interview:

> We will figure something out that seems relatively interesting and…spend some time in Northern Japan, talking to the master about how you can form metal in a certain way. As you truly understand that, that obviously informs your design, rather than it just being an arbitrary shape, that you annotate. The product architecture starts to become informed by your really understanding that material. That's an example of one of the reasons we don't do lots and lots of stuff, because that's time consuming and demanding.

Ive is describing what any good design student would understand as the basics of the craft. But his words are noteworthy for the two signature Apple notes he hits. The deep study and annotating are classic Apple. The implication is that the product will be ready when it's ready. Who will tell a samurai-sword master there's a ship deadline? Then there is his invocation of why "we don't do lots and lots of stuff." This is Apple's focus and its persistence in saying no, and it starts with the artist running industrial design.

Ive has an independent streak as well. Stocky, bald, and given to dark T-shirts, he is the only executive-team member to commute from San Francisco, where he lives with his wife, Heather, and twin sons. (Apple designers as well as many of its younger engineers and employees who work for the music-influenced iTunes group tend to be urban dwellers, not suburbanites.) Press accounts list famous friends who are design-oriented celebrities in their own right, often British, including the music world's DJ John Digweed and fashion designer Paul Smith. When the British screenwriter Alexander Chow-Stuart emailed a friend of a friend of Ive's in 2011 to ask if Chow-Stuart might say hello on a visit to Cupertino with his school-aged son, Ive not only obliged, but also gave the boy an iPod and arranged for a tour of the Apple campus. (Chow-Stuart lovingly recounted the visit on his personal blog.)

For a time it was fashionable for outsiders aware of his fame to speculate that Ive would replace Jobs as CEO. Apple insiders never took such talk seriously given Ive's avowed ignorance of business. After all, he'd had one taste of being a businessman running his own firm in London, and it didn't suit him. "I was terrible at running a design business, and I really wanted to just focus on the craft of design," he said. He clearly got this wish.

If Ive was never taken seriously internally as a potential CEO, one executive emerged in the last years of Steve Jobs's tenure at Apple who seemed he might have the critical elements needed to take the reins. His name is Scott James Forstall, a forty-three-year-old software engineer who specializes in user-interface design and has spent his entire career working for the two companies founded by Steve Jobs. *User interface* refers to the way computer users can manipulate what's on their screen. In many ways, the UI constitutes what's fun and useful about computers. Many consumers don't even notice UI, but the ease, elegance, and wit with which Apple users interact with their products is a key bond, hence the importance of Forstall's specialty.

Forstall, who is lean and swarthy, wears zip-up sweaters, and has a shock of black hair he styles to stick straight up in the air, grew up a naval brat in Washington State. He went to Stanford, where he studied symbolic systems as an undergraduate and earned a master's in computer science. He joined NeXT directly out of school. He moved to Apple in 1997 and worked for various senior Apple software executives over the years, developing a reputation as a smart and ambitious engineer, impatient to move up the ladder.

It wasn't until the development of the iPhone, though, that Forstall got his chance to shine internally. A team Forstall headed modified the software used by the Macintosh, OS X, to run on the iPhone. He ultimately became head of mobile software, an increasingly powerful job given the runaway success of the iPhone and the iPad. (Together with the iPod, these handheld devices accounted for almost 70 percent of Apple's revenue in 2011, compared with 20 percent for Macs.) In Apple's caste system, iOS devices are at the top of the heap. For example, more effort goes into modifying Macintosh applications like iLife for the iPad than for the Mac these days, adding to Forstall's institutional capital.

Forstall is praised for being brilliant, tough, a stickler for details, and unflappable. He keeps a jeweler's loupe in his office so he can look at every single pixel on every icon to make sure it's right. Simplicity in user-interface design is one of Forstall's great strengths. "He groks Steve's vision that way," observed an ex–Apple executive. (*Grok* is a slang term that first appeared in Robert Heinlein's sci-fi novel *Stranger in a Strange Land.* It means "to understand deeply through intuition or empathy.")

If there is a knock on Forstall, it's that he wears his ambition in plainer view than the typical Apple executive. He blatantly accumulated influence in recent years, including, it is whispered, when Jobs was on medical leave. He also accumulated the trappings of a captain of industry. For years he drove a beat-up Toyota Corolla, but with the wealth that came to all top managers at Apple in the 2000s, he eventually bought the same exact silver Mercedes coupe that Jobs drove. (Forstall could relate to Jobs in a more serious way, too. In the mid-2000s, he had a serious health scare, contracting a nasty stomach condition that forced him to be hospitalized, but from which he made a full recovery.)

Like Ive, Forstall has a life beyond Apple. He and his wife, Molly, a corporate lawyer, are huge fans of *American Idol* and have traveled to Los Angeles for the popular TV show's finale. Forstall is a rabid San Francisco Giants fan as well as a season-ticket holder for the Stanford women's basketball team. Toward the end of Jobs's tenure, Forstall began to get an increasing amount of airtime at Apple events, and ex-colleagues praise him as a top-notch speaker. In a company where so few executives even get the opportunity to show themselves to the public, Forstall's appearances were read by longtime Apple-watchers as having the same political significance that Cold War Kremlinologists ascribed to whoever was standing near Brezhnev on Lenin's Tomb. Forstall also has a leg up on his nerd colleagues with little public-speaking experience: He was an actor in his youth, having appeared in an Olympic High School theater troupe called Lalapalooza Bird that performed in several elementary schools in his hometown of Bremerton, Washington. As a senior, he played the title character in the Stephen Sondheim musical *Sweeney Todd*. He also has serious nerd cred in a town where Stanford engineers are the cool kids. As an undergraduate, Forstall was in the same fraternity, Phi Kappa Psi, as future Yahoo! co-founder Jerry Yang.

Eight years younger than Tim Cook, Forstall easily could be a CEO-in-waiting, especially if Apple's board decides it needs a CEO more in the image of Steve Jobs. Already he has had opportunities to move in influential Silicon Valley circles in a way that previously only Jobs would have. Because the ecosystem around iPhones and iPads has become so lucrative for Apple and the companies developing apps for it, Apple has grown increasingly willing to engage with the entrepreneurial world seeding those companies. Forstall, for example, spoke in 2011 to a group of mobile application companies funded by Kleiner Perkins, the influential venture capital firm. Matt Murphy, the Kleiner partner who runs its mobile applications–focused iFund, praises Forstall's "boyish enthusiasm" as well as his willingness to listen to suggestions from the entrepreneurs Murphy funds. The entrepreneurs seem to appreciate Forstall too. "He is a sharp, down-to-earth, and talented engineer, and a more than decent presenter," said one Kleiner-backed entrepreneur who has interacted with Forstall. "He's the total package."

A small handful of other senior executives completed the rest of the package under Jobs. Jeff Williams, Tim Cook's top lieutenant, took over as head of operations when Cook moved up. Williams is in many ways a doppelgänger for Cook. Both hail from the South. Both built their careers at IBM. Both received nighttime MBAs from Duke. Tall, lean, and gray-haired, like Cook, Williams was said by Apple executives to look so much like his boss that from behind they could be mistaken for each other. Bob Mansfield, who runs hardware engineering, is a stocky engineer who joined Apple in 1999 when the company where he worked, graphics chips maker Raycer Graphics, was purchased. Mansfield is quieter than his peers (though on par with Cook, his longtime boss), and though his title long was senior vice president of Mac hardware engineering, Mansfield is responsible for the guts of all devices, including iPods, iPhones, and iMacs.

The final product-oriented member of the executive team is Eddy Cue, long Apple's deal-making executive, but also the head of Internet services and for years Jobs's go-to guy for fixing problems. Cue led the initial negotiations with AT&T for the iPhone, for example. When Jobs needed a change atop Apple's MobileMe email service, he turned to Cue. Yet Jobs never promoted Cue to the top echelon of Apple. Elevating Cue was Cook's first publicly announced move—signaling that under Cook a "deal guy" could reach the inner circle of a product-oriented executive group.

What these people have in common is their length of service at Apple. The Apple culture is so tough that newcomers face long odds. Bob Mansfield has the shortest tenure, twelve years at the company. Scott Forstall worked with Steve Jobs since Forstall was fresh out of graduate school. If newcomers can succeed in the company's highest reaches, there isn't any recent evidence to prove it, and the one data point to consider suggests the contrary: the short, unhappy Apple career of Mark Papermaster.

In October 2008, Apple announced that it was hiring Papermaster, a veteran of IBM, to run the group that manufactured iPods and iPhones. Papermaster would be replacing Tony Fadell, the executive who ran the iPod team. Back then, Fadell had recently left Apple after repeated clashes with Jobs, among others. It seemed odd that Apple would turn to IBM for talent, and IBM was none too happy about Papermaster's hiring. It sued to try to prevent his joining Apple. It took until the following January to resolve the litigation, which allowed Papermaster to begin his work at Apple at the end of April, six months after he was hired.

Papermaster didn't last long, though, and the brevity of his tenure constitutes a cautionary tale for Apple's prospects at attracting senior managers in the future. Steve Jobs was on medical leave when Papermaster, who declined repeated requests to be interviewed, started at Apple. By the time Jobs returned, the word on Papermaster was that he wasn't fitting in. He wasn't seen as fighting hard for his division, a requisite internally. "Papermaster is a really nice guy, proverbially the guy you'd want to have a beer with," said someone who interacted with him during his time at Apple. "He is warm, patient, and willing to listen—just not the right qualities for Apple. It was so painfully obvious to everyone." It was said that when he came back to work, Jobs paid little attention to Papermaster, meaning the new executive had achieved "bozo" status in the founder's exacting judgment.

After Apple released its revamped iPhone 4, in June 2010, the company was hit by a raft of complaints over dropped calls, an episode dubbed "Antennagate" after Steve Jobs personally announced that the cause was a faulty antenna in the phone. (Jobs famously suggested that users weren't holding the phone correctly and then offered a rubber case to correct the problem.) Word leaked on August 7, 2010, that Papermaster, who oversaw the engineering of the phone, had quietly left Apple. He later reappeared as a vice president at Cisco, and, in late 2011, as chief technology officer at semiconductor maker AMD. Bob Mansfield added responsibility for devices engineering to his portfolio.

As CEO, Steve Jobs developed a loyal and able corps of lieutenants, a group he continued to direct up until nearly the last days of his life, despite having given up the chief executive's post. Jobs similarly dominated Apple's board of directors, even though he was its chairman only after stepping down as CEO.

The tale of Arthur Levitt's brief flirtation with joining the Apple board in 2001 illustrates how Jobs ran things. Levitt was nearing the end of his run as chairman of the Securities and Exchange Commission under Bill Clinton when Steve Jobs called to invite him to join the board. A committed Apple fan, Levitt was delighted. "I told him there's no board in America I'd rather join," Levitt recalled a decade later. Levitt flew to California, breakfasted with Jobs, met other members of the board, and attended Jobs's Macworld keynote at San Francisco's Moscone convention center. He received a board packet and a calendar of future board meetings and was excited about his first post-government assignment. Before he flew east, he left a copy of a recent speech he'd given on corporate governance with Fred Anderson, then Apple's chief financial officer.

When Levitt landed, there was a message waiting for him from Jobs. "I called him back, and he said he didn't think I'd be happy on the board," Levitt said. "He was effectively saying I was no longer wanted." Jobs didn't seem to like Levitt's opinion of what constituted good governance, including Levitt's opinion that board members should attend all meetings. Larry Ellison, an Apple board member at the time and a close friend of Jobs, had a poor attendance record. "He said I wouldn't be happy because his 'best director' didn't attend board meetings," said Levitt. "I was horribly disappointed."

Jobs's attitude toward Ellison, who left the board in 2002, citing his inability to attend board meetings, spoke volumes to his idea of board governance. Jobs continued to call Ellison his best director. He loved to tell the story of how he blew up the cover of a magazine with Ellison's face on it and placed the life-sized photo in an empty chair at Apple board meetings. "I'd turn to him and say, 'Larry, what do you think about that?'" Jobs recounted years later.

For years, Apple had no chairman, simply two "co-lead" directors, former Genentech CEO Art Levinson and former Intuit CEO Bill Campbell. The board had only six members other than the CEO, and many counted a connection to Jobs. Campbell was one of Jobs's closest friends and personal advisers, and he eventually relinquished his "lead" role because of the fiduciary need to disclose facts of Jobs's health he preferred not to discuss. Mickey Drexler had been CEO of the Gap, on whose board Jobs had served. Still, despite its personal connections to Jobs, Apple's board was considered first-rate based on the quality of its members. Andrea Jung, CEO of Avon Products, brought consumer experience and took Campbell's place as co-lead director. Al Gore, the former vice president, gave regulatory counsel—for years Jobs feared that Microsoft would stop supporting the Mac—and as an avid user of Apple's products became an eloquent advocate for the customer experience.

In his 2002 book *Take on the Street*, Levitt called Apple's board "highly qualified, prominent members of corporate America" but added that it nevertheless was "not designed to act independently of the CEO." He acknowledged that Apple had performed brilliantly in turning itself around. That was beside the point, however. "Small, insular boards lack the outside perspective that is necessary in case a company finds itself in trouble," concluded Levitt. "Especially when the CEO is as charismatic as Jobs, it's crucial to have independent thinkers who do not act as an extension of management."

No one would suggest that Apple is a company "in trouble." What's more, whether it was guided solely by

Jobs or not, the board thoroughly succeeded in fulfilling one of its key tasks by providing for an orderly succession at the top. Just as Apple won't truly be publicly tested until the products that were in the pipeline when Jobs died have been introduced, we won't learn the value of its board until the company faces its first crisis without its former leader.

6

Own Your Message

I first met Tim Cook on October 20, 2010, at an Apple product launch on the company's campus. Two years earlier, I had spent months working on an unauthorized profile of Cook that ran on the cover of *Fortune* magazine under the title, "The Genius Behind Steve: Could Operations Whiz Tim Cook Run the Company One Day?" No journalist had probed his background, career milestones, or personality as much as I had; yet I had never been granted an interview with him. I introduced myself to a smiling Cook. As we shook hands, I expected at least the slightest acknowledgment that this was our first time meeting each other, a nod or wink from him signifying something like, *Oh boy, I can't believe you called my Auburn classmates from the early 1980s and my old boss at IBM.*

I was mistaken. Personal chitchat was not on the agenda that day. It wasn't in the Apple script.

When Cook and I connected, I happened to be standing in the "demo room" after a press event dubbed "Back to the Mac" at which Apple unveiled a bevy of new computers. These events seem routine to the journalists who attend them, but they are not routine to the Apple employees who put them together. Each year there's an event for the iPhone, often to coincide with the annual Worldwide Developers Conference—WWDC in Applespeak. Another event showcases Apple's music offerings, often to highlight enhancements to iTunes or the iPod. iPad events are newer. The Mac event is a staple. These highly choreographed productions occur at one of about three locations: the massive Moscone Center in San Francisco, a more intimate theater at the nearby Yerba Buena Center for the Arts, or Apple's Town Hall auditorium in Infinite Loop 4 in Cupertino. The format is prescribed no matter the venue: a keynote address filled with demonstrations of whatever products and services are new, usually followed by an opportunity to see and play with the devices. In attendance typically will be journalists, investors, and partners, examples of the latter being cell phone companies for an iPhone event, game developers for an iPad event, and so on. But the focus is on the press, whose role is to rev up the blogosphere or start jawboning into the camera, explaining to the world the latest tricks up Apple's corporate sleeve.

On the day I encountered Cook, Apple had revealed its revolutionarily redesigned MacBook Air, a unibody, ultra-lightweight laptop computer. As an Apple news release enthused, the new computer was "an incredibly thin 0.11-inches at its thinnest point" and weighed "just 2.3 pounds." By chance, I was standing next to a chest-high display table holding a MacBook Air when Cook approached. Immediately he asked me what I thought of the computer. Unsure how to respond, I mumbled something about it being impressive. That was all he needed to launch into a short discourse on just how impressive the MacBook Air was. Its solid-state flash storage capacity that replaced the old disk drive—just like an iPad!—was fantastic. The new computer was super-thin, light, and fast as all get-out. It was like nothing else anybody had ever done before in the computer industry.

Cook and I chatted for a few minutes more as a minder from Apple's public relations staff hovered nearby, along with Phil Schiller, Apple's senior vice president of worldwide product marketing. Elsewhere in the room a frail-looking Steve Jobs held court with other journalists, reiterating the points about the MacBook Air he had made in his formal presentation and watched over by the head of Apple's PR department, Katie Cotton. A handful of other top executives mingled with the press, echoing the points Jobs and Cook were making about the laptop's magical new features.

The coordinated messaging was classic Apple, just one of countless examples of how Apple manages its image in a conscious, forceful, yet seemingly casual manner that nevertheless leaves absolutely nothing to chance. Messaging is another area where Apple goes its own way. The company breaks the mold when it comes to how it tells stories to consumers and how it treats information—no differently than it would silicon, titanium, or some other essential yet precious commodity. Call Apple's system Curate and Control.

Apple also brings its usual level of fanatical attention to

how it communicates to the outside world, but it employs different approaches depending upon the audience. With consumers, the message is ubiquitous but limited in scope. With journalists, information becomes a commodity that Apple doles out only after weighing the risk versus the potential return on investment. As part of its plan to debut, market, and sell each product, Apple decides who will speak about it and to whom, what the talking points will be, and which members of the press will be blessed with coveted interviews. The precise words Apple uses to communicate its message are repeated so many times that everyone, internally and externally, can recite them by heart.

The hallmarks of the Apple product message are, as with so much at Apple, simplicity and clarity. Throughout its history, Apple has unveiled products and features that either didn't previously exist in the industry or represented meaningful leaps forward. The simple design and capabilities of the first iPod and the groundbreaking multitouch expand-and-contract feature on the iPhone are two noteworthy examples.

The trick with selling breakthrough products is to explain them clearly. Bob Borchers, who was a senior product marketing executive for the iPhone, described Apple's approach to educating the public about the new product in 2007, when the smartphone market was dominated by BlackBerry and Palm. "When we launched the iPhone, it could have been a gazillion things," he recalled. "It did a huge number of functions and had multiple features." Rather than listing a multitude of capabilities, he said, Apple executives "boiled it down to three things: It was a revolutionary phone; it was the Internet in your pocket; and it was the best iPod we'd ever created."

The key, said Borchers, was highlighting exactly what made the iPhone stand out but giving consumers only as much as they needed to get excited. "If you compare that to any other mobile phone positioning in the market, it was unlike any of those devices," he said. "But this was the message that we rolled out in every piece of material that was in every briefing. It was everywhere."

It would be easy to dismiss this relentless repetition as creepily cultish, but this is just one of many ways that Apple achieves a brand identity that is the envy of any marketing professional. Consistency of message helps build customer loyalty. Clear messaging can also have a huge impact on the bottom line. "If there's one thing that I take away today, and I still use time and time again, it's that the best messaging is clear, concise, and repeated," reflected Borchers, who became a venture capitalist with the Silicon Valley firm Opus Capital after leaving Apple. "You're going to get tired of the message. You're going to do twenty briefings, and they'll all sound exactly the same to you. But that's what you want, because the person who is hearing it is hearing it for the first time. And where you get into trouble is where you start to mix it up because you're getting bored. So one of the key things was: Just use the same words over and over and over again. That will turn into the same words that the consumer hears, which ultimately will turn into the same words that they then use to define the product to their friends."

The happy outcome for Apple is that consumers don't feel played. Apple fanatics and industry pros may chuckle about the famous Steve Jobs "reality distortion field"— the founder's hypnotic ability to convince listeners of the goodness of whatever he happened to be pitching. But

for consumers, Apple has manufactured their reality. The
message comes at them from all directions, but it is easy
to understand. It feels organic, not forced. Yet make no
mistake: Apple planned the message's dissemination from
beginning to end.

Given that Apple is the ultimate top-down organization,
the art of corporate communications began at the top.
"Steve was a storyteller," reflected one departed executive.
"He could weave a story the company could get behind.
It's almost unheard of in a company that size." Executives
committed the corporate stories to memory long before
they began telling them to customers. That's because
they already had debated, vetted, tweaked, and tested the
story line repeatedly from the time Steve Jobs first told it
to them to the time they talked about it in public.

Storytelling may seem ephemeral and difficult to
quantify in a business setting, but George Blankenship,
a top executive of Apple's retail initiative when it began,
explained the very real link between storytelling and
driving demand. "If you went back to the year 2000 and
you looked at Apple, most people knew one thing about
Apple products: They didn't want one," he said. "And so
what ended up happening was an education process. We
needed to get in front of as many people as possible. So
they're walking by, and eventually one day they walk in.
And then we get a chance to tell the story and we tell that
story in a way that is respectful, helpful, friendly, and not
pushy. It's not about price. It's about product."

Like missionaries sent in diverse directions to proselytize, Apple executives have total recall for the message. "The goal of the Apple stores was to appeal to non-Macintosh customers," said Allen Olivo, a marketing executive at Apple when the stores opened, as if he had just conferred with Blankenship, which he hadn't. "We had to convince people who are skeptical, who don't use our products, who don't know what they can do with these products. When they walk in the store there has to be an experience that allows them to see and touch and feel and use and do stuff with the Mac."

Apple storytelling initially is high concept, telling customers not what they want to buy but what kind of people they want to be. This is classic "lifestyle" advertising, the selling of an image associated with a brand rather than the product itself. From Apple's iconic "Think Different" campaign in 1997 featuring images of Gandhi and Einstein and Bob Dylan (and no Apple products) to its later silhouetted hipsters grooving to music on their iPods (with the ubiquitous white earbuds connected to white cords streaking down their lithe bodies), Apple has excelled at selling a lifestyle.

Once Apple has the customer's attention, however, it goes to great lengths to explain in minute and gorgeous detail what its products can do. Consider the launch of a new version of its iMovie software in 2005. iMovie is one of several features in Apple's iLife software package, which is standard on Macs. (Whether you're aware of it or not, it sits there in the dock at the bottom of your screen. Its icon is a star reminiscent of those found on Hollywood's Walk of Fame.) Apple originally created iLife because so few third-party developers were writing programs for the

Mac. Supplying useful programs made the Mac more valuable, and explaining to customers how to use its software
became second nature to Apple.

In 2005, Apple introduced a high-definition version of
iMovie. Users could edit home movies on their Macs by
transferring video from handheld cameras onto their computers. High-def video cameras were just then becoming
widely available, so Apple confronted a chicken-and-egg
moment: It needed to demonstrate the value of HD video
in order to drive adoption of HD, which in turn justified
the value of its software and hardware.

One of the most common applications of iMovie had
been do-it-yourself wedding videos. Apple may not do
customer research to decide what products to make, but
it absolutely pays attention to how customers use its products. So the marketing team working on the iMovie HD
release scheduled for Macworld, on January 11, 2005,
decided to shoot a wedding. The ceremony it filmed
was gorgeous: a sophisticated, candlelit affair at the Offi-
cers' Club of San Francisco's Presidio. The bride was an
Apple employee, and the wedding was real. There was
one problem with the footage, however. Steve Jobs didn't
like it. He watched it the week before Christmas, recalled
Alessandra Ghini, the marketing executive managing
the launch of iLife. Jobs declared that the San Francisco
wedding didn't capture the right atmosphere to demonstrate what amateurs could do with iMovie. "He told us
he wanted a wedding on the beach, in Hawaii, or some
tropical location," said Ghini. "We had a few weeks to
find a wedding on a beach and to get it shot, edited, and
approved by Steve. The tight time frame allowed for no
margin for error."

With time short and money effectively no object, the team went into action. It contacted Los Angeles talent agencies as well as hotels in Hawaii to learn if they knew of any weddings planned—preferably featuring an attractive bride and groom—over the New Year's holiday. They hit pay dirt in Hollywood: A gorgeous agency client and her attractive fiancé were in fact planning to wed on Maui during the holiday. Apple offered to pay for the bride's flowers, to film the wedding, and to provide the couple with a video. In return, Apple wanted rights for up to a minute's worth of footage of its choosing.

Filming the event was no small production. An Apple creative director and crew flew to Hawaii. They worked with local florists to get the look they wanted. They also huddled repeatedly with the couple, who was understandably concerned by all the hubbub. A camera crew canvassed the beach the day before to make sure they understood where the sun would set. Shortly after the wedding, the director began uploading footage and called California with good news: "I'm super happy," he said. Steve Jobs was pleased, too. He approved the new footage a few days before Macworld. In the end, the Macworld keynote used a roughly sixty-second clip of the wedding, featuring sequences of the bride and groom kissing, the bride and her father dancing, and the newlywed couple strolling off into the sunset. Slightly longer versions ran during an on-site trailer at the event and in Apple retail stores. "The budget is significant," remembered Ghini, who nevertheless was unfazed by the expenditure. "It had to be because of the last-minute changes."

From Apple's perspective, the lavish spending is worth it because nothing is more valuable than the Apple brand.

It's a nuanced and subtle approach. Nine times out of ten, the distinctions will not consciously register with the typical consumer. But that's beside the point. The sum total of Apple's obsessions, including how it projects its image, absolutely is not lost on its customers, who intuitively appreciate that Apple is a cut above. This explains why no one at Apple thinks it's the slightest bit unusual to hire the London Symphony Orchestra to record iMovie music trailers.

And nobody bats an eye at big outlays that end up being for naught. When Apple was preparing to launch the version of its Macintosh operating system called Snow Leopard, the marketing team had planned to use a stock photo of an elusive cat but wanted to try to do better. The group sent a crew to photograph a snow leopard in captivity—at considerable expense. Steve Jobs wasn't satisfied with the result. "He looks fat and lazy," said Jobs. "Not hungry and fast."

The lights go down. The crowd hushes itself with anticipation. Music that has been blaring, typically a popular anthem, an old U2 song perhaps, fades. Steve Jobs walks onstage, and the crowd goes wild. Senior Apple executives sit in the first couple of rows, joined by VIPs like venture capitalist John Doerr or Apple board member Al Gore. They clap and laugh and cheer along with everyone else. In Cupertino, Apple employees gather in cafeterias to watch on closed-circuit TVs. Given Apple's secrecy, what the public is about to see in an auditorium and what online viewers will watch on their iPads will be completely new to them—and just as new to Apple's employees. Even those who've worked on a portion of an about-to-be-launched product won't necessarily have a clue about what else will be announced simultaneously. They only know their portion.

This is an Apple keynote address. Steve Jobs described marketing as the cover of the Apple book, with products being what's on the pages inside. Just as products are the result of nearly endless design and manufacturing iterations, the keynote address is the highly honed presentation whereby Apple introduces to the world the fruits of its labor.

Jobs made an art form of keynotes, a stylized form of performance art that required contributions from the entire company. In the same way the different components of a jumbo jet are manufactured around the world and then assembled in a giant factory at the end of an arduous process, so, too, are Apple keynotes obsessively crafted in segments and then cobbled together for a massive audience on opening day.

Onstage, the keynote is a long collection of seemingly off-the-cuff remarks and live demonstrations. Behind the stage, Apple employees are a wreck. They've been rehearsing for months, leaving nothing to chance, assembling slides and photos and talking points to be whittled down into the presentation that is going on right now. (The slides will be in Apple's Keynote presentation software, of course, introduced in 2003 as Apple's answer to Microsoft's PowerPoint. The software grew out of a program Jobs had been using for just this purpose.) For a Mac event, Jobs worked off a Mac on a cart onstage. Offstage, an identical cart carried an identical Mac with the identical presentation on it in case the first one crashed.

Jobs himself rehearsed the presentation dozens of times so that each relaxed statement would come off just right. Partners, too, will have run through multiple rehearsals, all according to Apple's schedule and following Apple's script. One partner executive—Apple invites companies whose software works on Apple products to demonstrate their wares to buttress Apple's offerings—recounted spending a week and a half in Cupertino leading up to an Apple product launch. He presented to an increasingly senior list of Apple executives, culminating with Jobs. An aide to another high-profile executive who debuted software that ran on Apple's iPhone recalled the marching orders: "They told us—didn't ask us, told us—what time the rehearsal was, what he should wear, and what he should say. There was no discussion about it."

A keynote will cycle through a handful of products. For years Jobs did the entire presentation himself, with bit roles played by low-level employees brought onstage to demonstrate features. Over time, other executives took on more and more prominent roles. The signature finale to a major keynote speech is the slide that appears saying, ONE MORE THING...—signifying something important, new, and exciting. (The iPod Shuffle in 2005, the fifteen-inch MacBook Pro in 2006, and a dramatically revamped MacBook Air in 2010 are some examples.) Music product events will conclude with a performance by a big-name recording artist, like John Mayer or Coldplay's Chris Martin. In 2009, a tentative Norah Jones sang two songs to conclude an iTunes event, obviously rattled by Apple's neurotic pre-gig machinations. "There's lots of secret passageways back there, secret door-knocks," she said, an electric guitar hanging from her neck. "I feel like a burden's been lifted now that we can play." She added, "Just kidding," though clearly she wasn't. After Jones strummed her last note, Jobs came out and pecked her on the cheek.

When the crowds are gone and the briefings are over, Apple employees will repair to one of a handful of nearby watering holes, like the XYZ Bar at the W Hotel across the street from the Moscone Center, to unwind. Many will immediately take vacations. They know the work on the next keynote will begin as soon as they return.

Apple's marketing and communications team works in a building just across from 1 Infinite Loop called M-3, the *M* standing for "Mariani Avenue," not for marketing. When the marketers walk through the front door and then two consecutive secured doors, they walk around a light blue wall to get to their desks. On the wall is painted a prominent message in large whitish silver letters. It reads: SIMPLIFY, SIMPLIFY, SIMPLIFY. A broad line is drawn through the first two SIMPLIFYS.

It is not just Apple's products that are fiercely simple, but also the way it deploys its brand. Consider the boilerplate language that appears at the bottom of every press release Apple issues. A version from late 2011 read: "Apple designs Macs, the best personal computers in the world, along with OS X, iLife, iWork and professional software. Apple leads the digital music revolution with its iPods and iTunes online store. Apple has reinvented the mobile phone with its revolutionary iPhone and App Store, and has recently introduced iPad 2 which is defining the future of mobile media and computing devices." That's it. Three sentences to describe $108 billion in revenue. Each word is carefully chosen. *Design* is the first verb. Macs come first because, after all, Macs came first. Apple "leads" and "reinvents." It is "revolutionary" (twice), and is nothing if not about the "future." The wording is conscious and deliberate. *"Revolutionize,"* said a former Apple marketer, "may be the most used word in Apple marketing."

The company is just as careful about how the Apple brand is used. Nobody has blanket permission to use it, first of all, and that includes insiders. A consultant who put the logo on his website to show that Apple was a client was asked to take it down. People who buy Apple products, on the other hand, are encouraged to display the Apple logo: Inside its product packaging Apple includes stickers with the iconic apple, which have a way of showing up on everything from spiral notebooks to car bumpers to refrigerators.

The message is driven home to employees who deal with the outside world. "You don't want anything to detract from the brand," said Lars Albright, an executive in Apple's iAd mobile advertising business who left Apple in 2011 and founded SessionM, a start-up that helps applications developers retain their users. "And that's in every aspect of it. You think through the lens of 'Would this jeopardize the brand? Do we need to do it? Is it too much of a risk?'"

Apple's brand czar, Hiroki Asai, is a quiet executive almost completely unknown to the general public. He studied printed design at California Polytechnic State University, where Mary LaPorte, his graphic design professor, remembered him as a stickler for details and aesthetic integrity. "If he wanted a coffee cup stain on a poster, then he would make sure it was coffee, and not brown ink," she recalled.

After college, he worked at a consulting firm in San Francisco, where Pixar and later Apple were clients. He joined Apple in 2001, ultimately reported directly to Steve Jobs, and is considered the final word on every piece of marketing material except for advertising. His domain, as explained in his Cal Poly bio, provides another piece of insight into the Apple penchant for integration. "With over 200 creatives under his supervision, his team has been responsible for all of the packaging, retail store graphics, website, on-line store, direct marketing, videos, and event graphics for Apple globally for the past decade," the bio reads. "His team is a combination of Art Directors, Writers, Motion Graphic Designers, Developers, and Designers... The team is unique in that it is the only one of its size that can design, produce, and engineer all of the communications work from every creative discipline all in-house." Inside Apple, Asai is known as a silent force who understood what Jobs thought about the Apple brand and knew, said one colleague, "how to channel Steve." Asai also is known for his youthful appearance. Said an executive who worked with him: "He looks like he just got out of third-period design class."

As for advertising, Apple had a distinctive approach under Steve Jobs. He considered advertising a key part of marketing, and he managed it himself. He met weekly with Lee Clow, the creative director for TBWA\Chiat\Day, Apple's longtime agency. Jobs also took a direct interest in where the ads ran. He favored TV shows that fit the sensibility of Apple's perceived customer. *Modern Family*, *The Daily Show*, and *Family Guy* were favorites. Smarter reality TV like *The Amazing Race* was preferred over the more mean-spirited *Survivor*. Jobs once flew off into a rage when an Apple spot accidentally found its way onto Glenn Beck's program on the Fox News Channel. Jobs detested Fox News, but he generally didn't want Apple to advertise on any political talking-head show.

Jobs remained a believer in print media even as his devices, especially the iPad, were hastening print's demise. Jobs was particularly enamored with Apple's full-page ads being positioned on the back covers of major magazines. Pick up a popular magazine to this day, and you'll likely see an Apple ad on the back. Monica Karo, the executive at OMD charged with buying ads on Apple's behalf, would periodically attempt to convince Jobs to run ads in new publications. Jobs, the master of publicity, had a stock response: "You worry about the back covers," he said. "I'll take care of the front covers."

So it's clear, front covers can't be purchased, at least not in respectable publications. But they are extremely valuable to marketers. Jobs knew better than any business executive in the world how to land himself on the front cover to promote a product. Apple also gets free publicity when its products appear in popular TV shows and films. The company says it never pays for product placement, but in 2010 Apple products appeared 386 times in original broadcast programs, according to Nielsen.

Such publicity is priceless, of course. Shortly before the iPad was released, the company agreed to provide two working units to the hit ABC sitcom *Modern Family*, which built an entire episode around geek-dad Phil Dunphy's earnest yearning for an iPad, which just happened to be released on his birthday. "It's like Steve Jobs and God got together to say 'We love you, Phil,'" the character said.

Apple's built-in advantage is that the creative set uses Apple's products. "I happen to be an Apple enthusiast and a big gadget freak, so I'm up on this stuff," said Steve Levitan, the co-creator of *Modern Family*. "The only product I've ever waited in line for was an iPhone." Levitan said the idea for the iPad episode originated creatively. "We're very selective. We tend to use these products when we want to use them anyway." He said the creative team was excited to learn that Jobs was a fan of the show. Levitan once arranged to travel to Northern California to meet Jobs, but the meeting fell through. He subsequently dealt regularly with the two Apple executives who are among the best known in Hollywood: iTunes chief Eddy Cue and Suzanne Lindbergh, Apple's New York–based head of product placements. Lindbergh must also have the coolest title of any Apple honcho: "director buzz."

One of Apple's most potent storytelling tools is its muscular use of public relations. Once again, it's an example of Apple disregarding all the normal rules of corporate life. For Apple, PR is as carefully managed, tight-lipped, and unforgiving as its approach to product design and internal secrecy.

Indeed, Apple thinks different(ly) about something as mundane as who speaks for Apple. When Apple launched the iPhone in 2007, precisely five people were authorized to speak to the press about it: Steve Jobs, Tim Cook, Phil Schiller, Greg Joswiak, and Bob Borchers. Joswiak was the vice president for iPhone product marketing, and Borchers worked for him. The two most senior product executives who built the iPhone, hardware boss Tony Fadell and

Scott Forstall, whose team developed the software, were not on that list—and were none too happy, per Borchers, to be excluded from the victory lap in the media.

As the lowest-ranking member of the approved group, Borchers explained the mentality of restricting even senior executives from speaking. "The challenge with those guys is that they're super smart and they know a lot of details, but they haven't spent a lot of time in front of the press," he said. "They're likely to get asked questions that they know the answers to but that they haven't learned how to gracefully avoid answering."

Apple's public relations department operates not so much on a need-to-know basis as a you-will-not-know basis. It may be the one corner of the company that has most mastered the art of saying no. Members of the PR team have specific assignments, typically organized around product areas. Product is the one subject about which Apple's PR group will talk, especially to repeat factual information about products in the marketplace. Off-limits questions include unreleased products, personal information about Apple executives, details about future Apple events, and pretty much anything about the inner workings of the company. In a phone call or meeting with an Apple publicist, a journalist is far more likely to be probed for information about upcoming coverage than to be the recipient of anything of value.

Apple's PR strategy with journalists, hobbyists, and careerists from every corner of the earth is to be extremely judicious about doling out information. It's a posture almost no other company can take. The norm in the corporate world is for public relations professionals to maintain relationships with reporters. They schmooze them, flatter them, feed them tidbits—not to mention food and drink—keep abreast of their personal lives, and invite them into the company for periodic updates from senior management.

Apple plays this game only at the highest levels. Katie Cotton, its powerful vice president of worldwide communications, runs the PR apparatus. A slender, sharp-elbowed forty-six-year-old, Cotton worked in the 1990s at a PR agency in Los Angeles, KillerApp Communications, where she represented nascent digital entertainment companies like RealNetworks and Virgin Interactive Entertainment. The agency did work for NeXT, though Cotton did not, and through connections in the Apple-NeXT orbit she ended up at Apple in 1996. Rising to the top of the PR ranks, Cotton ultimately reported directly to Steve Jobs and fiercely guarded his privacy, barring the door to all but a handful of reporters. A gatekeeper for the outside world, she is the enforcer internally, too, coming down hard on any Apple employee, almost no matter how senior, with the mistaken impression that he or she is allowed to speak on behalf of Apple. In a world of men for whom a clean pair of blue jeans counts as business attire, Cotton stands out for her style; her Alexander Wang dresses and shoes are far more Manhattan than San Jose.

Under Cotton's regime, Apple's approach makes it no place to learn PR—because PR at Apple is mostly a one-way street. Publicists at other companies, accustomed to a large measure of sycophantism toward journalists and their clients, are fascinated by the undiplomatic ways of Apple. "They are highly aggressive and communicative when they want something from you," reflected a publicist for a major technology company that is an Apple partner. "But the moment you're no longer needed, it's as if you didn't exist anymore. They'll literally stop returning phone calls. Nobody else can do that."

Apple PR does play favorites. Reporters and editors from a handful of cherished publications with long relationships with the company, *Fortune* magazine among them, enjoy preferential treatment. This is especially true around product launches, when Apple will negotiate exclusive access in return for prominent placement—the front covers Jobs bragged about handling himself. iTunes, for example, was unveiled on the cover of *Fortune* in 2003, featuring a photo of Jobs with the singer Sheryl Crow. The previous year Apple blessed *Time* with an exclusive look at the first flat-panel iMac, with Jobs grinning on a sleek display next to the headline "Flat-out Cool!"

Investors fare no differently with Apple. The company's two-person investor-relations team doles out precious little information to Wall Street analysts and shareholders, in a way that is unlike any other company's. Apple holds no analyst day, a routine event at most companies that exposes several hundred investors to upper management, who make presentations about the company's plans. Jobs treated investors with something between ambivalence and contempt. "He was the only CEO I knew who didn't meet with investors," said Toni Sacconaghi of Sanford Bernstein. "You could be a shareholder with $2 billion worth of stock for five years and never have met Steve Jobs." Sacconaghi viewed the Apple management team as nearly useless in trying to probe for information, with one exception. "Tim Cook is the only one who would provide some color that was unscripted," he said.

There is an exception to the rule when it comes to Apple's communications with the public. Apple actively caters to (as opposed to dictates to) influential product reviewers. Two particularly matter: David Pogue of the *New York Times* and Walt Mossberg of the *Wall Street Journal*. A former Apple iTunes engineer remembered being called at home shortly after his first child was born. "David Pogue's Apple TV was crashing," the engineer said, referring to the witty and widely read gadget critic. "They wanted me to go through the development logs of David Pogue's Apple TV. I'm like, 'You're kidding, right?' Because what happens is that when there's a fire, if you want to get it out as fast as possible, you call every single expert. Apple TV was getting ready to release and Apple is very concerned about public perception."

Pogue, who also writes well-regarded and exceptionally wonky how-to books for computer users, is a key influencer. But no journalist is as important to Apple's public perception as Walt Mossberg. (In personal-technology circles, the name Walt is nearly as well known as Steve.) A former defense correspondent, Mossberg fashioned himself into the most influential personal-technology critic in the United States by advocating for average consumers, of which he considered himself one. Throughout the second reign of Steve Jobs, Mossberg was a stalwart proponent of Apple's products, an unabashed cheerleader for Apple's ease of use and technical superiority over the blandness and complexity of the Microsoft-dominated PC. Jobs rewarded Mossberg with rare appearances at the technology conference Mossberg ran with the Silicon Valley journalist Kara Swisher, All Things Digital.

If Mossberg disapproved of an Apple product, there
was no question whose side Jobs would take. In 2008,
when Mossberg, along with many other critics, panned
MobileMe, an email synchronization service that was supposed to mimic the functionality offered by the popular
BlackBerry smartphone, Jobs erupted. He called a meeting of the MobileMe team and berated them for having
disappointed him, themselves, and one another. Worst
of all, they had embarrassed Apple publicly. "You've tar-
nished Apple's reputation," he told them. "You should hate
each other for having let each other down. Walt Mossberg,
our friend, is no longer writing good things about us."

Celebrities of all kinds get red-carpet treatment at
Apple, which is well aware that pleasing public figures
is textbook image management. Steve Doil, an executive
in Apple's operations group in the mid-2000s, tells of the
request that found its way to him when the crooner Harry
Connick Jr. needed a new monitor for his Mac. "It was
my first escalation," he said, referring to Apple's process
for elevating a typical customer-service request for a VIP.
Connick had sent an email to Jobs, said Doil, who for-
warded the note to Cook, who passed it along to Deirdre
O'Brien, a top procurement executive. "She told me, 'This
is your first Steve request. Don't disappoint.'" Doil dis-
patched the monitor in thirty-five minutes.

Apple's approach to PR is unique, but it isn't unprec-
edented. In fact, Jobs's canny behavior as pitchman to
the public and flatterer of influential scribes evokes the
model set by one of his heroes, Edwin Land, inventor of
the Polaroid camera. Decades before Jobs spun a vision of
Apple and its products, Land mastered the art of corporate

promotion at Polaroid. He staged showy events to reveal big products. Land made sure that reporters for mainstream publications covered his events in addition to the industry journalists who could be relied on to show up. When he unveiled his system for instant photography in 1947, for example, Land invited the *New York Herald Tribune* along with *National Photo Dealer* for his talk to the Optical Society of America. Like Jobs, Land had a special fondness for *Fortune*, according to Land's biographer, Victor McElheny, author of a tome whose title easily could be an epitaph for Jobs: *Insisting on the Impossible*. McElheny noted that Land was so good at promotion, his inventions were featured in popular museum exhibits even as he was commercializing them. "He understood publicity," said McElheny.

Jobs never said whether or not he learned his promotional wizardry by studying Land. He made no secret of his admiration, however. He visited the great man in 1983, after he had been fired from Polaroid. According to former Apple CEO John Sculley, who visited Land with Jobs, the two bonded over their shared ability to envision world-changing products before the products had been built. A few years later Jobs rhapsodized about Land in an interview with *Playboy*. "Land was a troublemaker," Jobs said. "He dropped out of Harvard and founded Polaroid. Not only was he one of the great inventors of our time but, more important, he saw the intersection of art and science and business and built an organization to reflect that." He called the Polaroid board's decision to kick Land out of his own company "one of the dumbest things I've ever heard of." Jobs kept thinking about Land for years and from time to time would bring him up, unbidden, still smarting at the lack of appreciation for one of the world's great entrepreneurs and storytellers.

It isn't just with the press that Apple carefully restricts access. Apple is just as selfish about lending its time or name to another company's marketing efforts. It's rare to see an Apple executive appear at a non-Apple product event and even rarer to find an independent academic who has studied Apple with Apple's cooperation. The world's most discussed company may well be the least observed, at least from the inside.

One academic who has analyzed Apple, Harvard Business School's David Yoffie, is almost wistful about the subject. Yoffie teaches courses on strategy, technology, and international competition, topics that increasingly can't be mastered without a deep knowledge of Apple. Indeed, Yoffie, who has been on the Harvard faculty since 1981, once was the academic world's foremost authority on Apple, having roamed the halls freely in the early 1990s. "For my first case study on Apple, [then-CEO John] Sculley gave me total access for six to eight months, including tons of internal interviews," Yoffie said.

Over time, Yoffie's relationship with Apple grew complicated, leading to Steve Jobs having "mixed feelings" about him. Yoffie joined the board of Intel in 1989, yet he continued to comment publicly on various companies wearing his Harvard hat. "I was very critical of Apple in the 1997 to 2000 time frame," he recalled, and he eventually fell victim to the "long memory" of Steve Jobs. As Apple's fortunes improved, including after Apple shifted to Intel chips for its Macintosh computers, Yoffie remained in the doghouse, despite having "changed my tune" and begun commenting positively on Apple. Said Yoffie: "[Jobs] said he'd be willing to let me come in once Intel and Apple had a formal relationship. Then he said, 'No. You've been too critical.'"

In September 2010, Yoffie published an update on his Apple case study, his eighth revision since his first case when John Sculley was CEO. In reviewing Apple's entire history, the case begins with a recent summary, gushing that "by almost any measure, Apple's turnaround was a spectacular accomplishment." Over the years Yoffie had become a tech-industry insider, serving on the boards of TiVo, Financial Engines, and Apple competitor HTC, in addition to Intel. For all his industry knowledge, Yoffie's Apple case study doesn't contain a shred of original information. (He acknowledged the lack of new material, though he also noted that the paper won the European Case Clearing House award for best case study in 2011.)

Yoffie certainly isn't alone among academics shut out of Apple. Theoretical physicist Geoffrey West is the past president of the Santa Fe Institute and a darling of Silicon Valley intellectuals. He has devoted his recent research to the life and death of corporations. To his chagrin, Apple isn't in his field of observation. "I have no knowledge of Apple as a company," he said. "I only know I love their products. In my work Google pops up all the time. I almost never hear anyone talk about Apple in academic terms. Unlike Google and Amazon, I don't even know anyone who works at Apple."

7

Overwhelm Friends/Dominate Foes

Long before unveiling its first smartphone on January 9, 2007, executives at Apple already knew what they wanted to call the device.

The iPod music player, which launched on October 23, 2001, had in four years' time become a nearly $8 billion business. The iTunes Store, Apple's online pop-culture dispensary where consumers could purchase music, movies, and TV shows, had opened for business on April 28, 2003. It was generating annual revenues of almost $2 billion as Apple readied its smartphone. Obviously, the new device should be called "iPhone."

One problem: The name iPhone already had an owner, the giant Silicon Valley company Cisco Systems.

The businesses of Apple and Cisco barely overlapped. Cisco made equipment that allowed big businesses and telephone companies to connect to the Internet. That equipment—routers, switches, and other gear a consumer would never know anything about—is often referred to as the plumbing of the Internet. Cisco did own a small home-networking business, Linksys, and it later would stumble by paying $533 million for the maker of Flip video cameras, a product Apple would help put out of business—with, of all things, the capabilities of the iPhone. But on the eve of the launch of the iPhone, Cisco and Apple would barely have competed with each other. Both were prominent Silicon Valley neighbors. Cisco targeted businesses, Apple consumers.

In 2000, Cisco had acquired InfoGear, an Israeli company that had a product called an iPhone, which it had trademarked in 1996. This was before Apple started slapping an *i* in front of its product names, beginning with the iMac in 1998. Jobs never said exactly what the letter stood for, though in the iMac introduction he displayed a slide that read: "internet, individual, instruct, inform, inspire." The many later *i*-labeled products never illuminated the meaning of the *i*. It just became Apple's naming tic.

For Cisco's part, the *i* actually meant something: It was selling a line of phones to companies that worked off the Internet, as opposed to Ma Bell's system. Cisco had discontinued the original InfoGear product, but its Linksys division had begun using the name, according to Charles Giancarlo, a senior Cisco executive at the time. As Apple ramped up planning for its smartphone release, it called to inform Cisco that it would be naming its new product, for which it had high hopes, the iPhone.

Giancarlo fielded a call directly from Steve Jobs. "Steve called in and said that he wanted it," Giancarlo recalled. "He didn't offer us anything for it. It was just like a promise he'd be our best friend. And we said, 'No, we're planning on using it.'" Shortly after that, Apple's legal department called to say they thought Cisco had "abandoned the brand," meaning that in Apple's legal opinion Cisco hadn't adequately defended its intellectual property rights by promoting the name. To Apple's way of thinking this meant the name iPhone was available for Apple's use. Giancarlo, who subsequently joined the prominent Silicon Valley private-equity firm Silver Lake Partners, said Cisco threatened litigation before the launch. Then, the day after Apple announced its iPhone, Cisco filed suit.

The negotiation displayed some classic Steve Jobs negotiating tactics. Giancarlo said Jobs called him at home at dinnertime on Valentine's Day, as the two sides were haggling. Jobs talked for a while, Giancarlo related. "And then he said to me, 'Can you get email at home?'" Giancarlo was taken aback. This was 2007, after all, when broadband Internet was ubiquitous in homes in the US, let alone that of a Silicon Valley executive who had worked for years on advanced Internet technology. "And he's asking me if I'm able to get email at home. You know he's just trying to press my buttons—in the nicest possible way." Cisco gave up the fight shortly after that. The two sides reached a vague agreement to cooperate on areas of mutual interest.

Giancarlo had been considered a candidate to replace John Chambers as CEO, and when he resigned from Cisco later that year, he witnessed the other side of Steve Jobs. Their frequent correspondence had stopped cold as soon as Cisco and Apple had agreed on terms, but Jobs called immediately when he heard of Giancarlo's departure. Jobs, a charmer and master networker, wished him well in a way that conveyed total sincerity. Said Giancarlo: "You could have knocked me over with a feather."

Apple would again ride roughshod over Cisco three years later when Apple decided that it wanted a new name for its mobile operating system, heretofore the "iPhone OS." For nearly twenty years, Cisco had been referring to the core operating system for its equipment as IOS, for "Internet Operating System," though the product had been fragmented by other offerings. The second time around Apple was more cordial if no less matter of fact with Cisco before taking the name for its own. This time the two companies reached a deal before Apple went public with the new name. Apple debuted its renamed iOS when Jobs unveiled the iPhone 4 in June 2010. Recalled an executive who was involved in the Apple-Cisco negotiations: "Jobs basically did what he wanted."

From the time Apple first lost its momentum, in the early 1990s, until it started to branch out beyond computers in the early 2000s, the company operated in an odd world of isolation. Its hardware was different, its software worked differently, and its market share was small. Apple ran apart from the rest of Silicon Valley, maintaining an underdog mentality well after it ceased being an underdog. Apple also had a long corporate memory: It harbored grudges from the time software developers shunned the Macintosh. In its darkest days, when Apple was dangerously close to being irrelevant, its institutional psyche retained the pride of having pioneered the personal computer. Even a down-trodden Apple thought of itself as more stylish than the beige world of Wintel PCs—the powerful combination of Windows software powered by Intel chips. Even after it regained its record for success, Apple retained the aloof, and often arrogant, bearing of an outsider.

Arguably because Apple did things its own way, forging a business model that is unique in so many ways, Apple also institutionalized a culture of playing by its own rules. Partners of all types, from suppliers to consultants to collaborators, find out soon enough that Apple's playbook is the only one that matters.

It is one thing for a company to maintain an alternative culture within its own walls—an absolute monarch can usually control what happens in his own kingdom—but what happens when that value system, that way of doing business, comes into contact with other entities? These interactions often reveal the strengths and weaknesses of a company's own operating system. Time and again, Apple has made being fed at a special table part of its business model, whether it is dealing with dinosaurs of old media in the music, movie, and publishing industries, partners in the telecommunications world, or suppliers who provide it with raw materials to manufacture their goods.

Apple has redefined the rules wherever it pleased. Its iTunes Store told music publishers what they could and couldn't charge for songs. In exchange for two years of exclusivity on the iPhone, Apple told AT&T that Apple, and not the phone carrier, would control the user experience and even the branding on the phone—a reversal for the cellular business. Dissatisfied with the job Best Buy salespeople were doing selling Apple's wares, Apple put its own employees into Best Buy stores. The retailer swallowed hard and effectively thanked Apple for its business. Application developers whine about the opaque approval process for getting an app onto Apple's App Store. But they continue submitting applications: By late 2011, the App Store had five hundred thousand apps and Apple had paid its developers $3 billion in sales revenue in three years—despite dictating another rigid set of terms, that Apple would always take a 30 percent cut and maintain total control over what went into its store.

As for its dealings with suppliers, what other companies might think of as valued business partners, Apple calls to mind how the United States "consulted" with NATO during the Cold War. Yes, there was an alliance. But there was only one superpower. Apple thinks nothing of sending a twenty-something-year-old engineer to Asia to explain to experienced manufacturers precisely how Apple wants something made. This simply is how Apple treats partners, loosely defined, of all stripes. "There is no such thing as a partnership with Apple," said a former Apple executive. "It's all about Apple."

Whether it is textbook maverick behavior, an arrogance bred from success, or the consequence of being led for years by Steve Jobs, Apple decides when and how it will play with others. Jobs, after all, regularly parked in the handicapped parking place (while healthy) at Apple. He removed the license plates from his car for fear of being tracked. Bob Borchers, the former Apple marketing executive, offered as an example the way a typical Steve Jobs keynote presentation used the logos of other companies. "He always ended up doing a white logo on a black background"—in other words, the way Apple presents its own logo. "In many cases that is not within the brand guidelines for the partner, and in many cases the brand guidelines mandate that you have to have the circle-R, the copyright logo. That always gets cropped out because it's just unsightly." It is behavior Jobs wouldn't have tolerated from another company—a violation of Apple's branding rules is unforgivable—yet he didn't even consider asking permission for his own presentations.

If Apple is rough with its friends, suffice it to say it is positively devilish with its enemies.

Its "Get a Mac" ad campaign, which ran from 2006 to 2009, stands out for its nastiness and brutality, a full-frontal assault on a competitor in an industry that typically stresses strengths over comparisons. If McDonald's had attacked Burger King or Ford attacked Chrysler in such a way, audiences might have recoiled in horror, yet Apple was able to get away with this public ridicule.

Prior to "Get a Mac," Apple's advertising traditionally followed three models: edgy (the *1984*-inspired spots), warm and fuzzy (happy people doing fun things with Apple products), and hardware porn (a camera slowly rotating around a gorgeous device). This campaign, widely known as "Mac vs. PC," set a new tone for Apple: mean-spirited, couched in warm and fuzzy.

The campaign, created by Apple's longtime agency, TBWA\Media Arts Lab, relentlessly sent the message that Macs were cool, hip, safe, simple to use, elegant, and otherwise delightful, while PCs were nerdy, old, virus-ridden, complicated, awkward, and generally a chore to use. With the famous line, "Hi, I'm a Mac," the slim, genial actor Justin Long, boyfriend of child-star-turned-legit-adult-actress Drew Barrymore, portrayed all that was good about the Macintosh. To personify the PC, a proxy for Microsoft, which supplies the software, the ads turned to John Hodg-man, the portly, nerdy, sloppily and unfashionably dressed, and hapless actor and comedian best known for his work on *The Daily Show.* In spot after spot, the cool Mac bested the pitiable PC. The PC got tied up in its own power cords; that wouldn't happen on a Mac, which uses an elegant magnet system to connect. The PC needed a hazmat suit to protect itself from computer viruses; hackers didn't attack Macs. Another added a faux Microsoft publicist to defend Vista, the dud of an iteration to Windows that Microsoft unveiled in 2007. The PR woman had "no comment" to Mac's contention that Vista was causing PC users to switch to Macs.

The taunting got so vicious that Microsoft had no choice but to respond. It hired the edgy ad agency Crispin Porter + Bogusky to create a campaign called "I'm a PC." The goal was to remind PC users—there are about a bil-lion of them—that Apple's broadsides had become per-sonal and that Microsoft wasn't the only party that should be offended. "Over time it became clear they were begin-ning to insult some of our customers," said David Web-ster, Microsoft's general manager of brand and marketing strategy. "It's okay to insult our products, but our cus-tomers said: 'We're not losers.' " After initially, and awk-wardly, pairing Bill Gates with Jerry Seinfeld, Microsoft's ads turned to real PC users, each of whom was easier on the eyes than John Hodgman. Microsoft later would claim that its counterattack forced Apple to abandon the assault. It's just as likely Apple felt it was done making its devas-tating point—the schoolyard bully who stops when his arm gets tired of punching.

As Apple has shifted from underdog to top dog, it hasn't

ameliorated its sharp edge. Tim Cook publicly threatened litigation against tiny Palm, then headed by ex–Apple hardware honcho Jon Rubinstein, when Palm debuted a new smartphone that had many of the best characteristics of an iPhone. The episode was a blip because the Palm Pre flopped with consumers, and Palm quickly sold itself to HP. Yet the burst of pique offers a tiny window into Apple's thin-skinned soul. Rubinstein was the rare ex–Apple executive with the audacity to come directly after Apple. The new smartphone enjoyed a moment in the sun when product reviewers praised some of its snazzier features, which not even the iPhone could best. By any objective measure Palm was never a threat to Apple. Yet Apple has a take-no-prisoners mind-set. It doesn't tolerate mediocrity on the inside, and it fights viciously against perceived wrongs on the outside. In his calm-toned repartee, Cook showed his bite to be as sharp as Jobs's.

Copying Apple was certain to enrage Jobs, which was ironic to students of Silicon Valley history given Apple's appropriation of inventions from the likes of Xerox PARC and others. Jobs was furious with Google after it began supplying its Android mobile operating system to cell phone makers. Near the end of his life he praised Microsoft's latest mobile software offerings for being original. "At least they didn't copy us the way Google did," he said. He also famously attacked Adobe, a longtime Apple partner, by refusing to allow its Flash media player to run on iPads—and then saying publicly that Flash was an inferior product. We'll never know if Apple truly found Flash technologically lacking or if Jobs considered the move payback for Adobe's decision a decade earlier not to produce Macintosh versions of its key products. In 2011, Apple waged a multinational patent battle against Samsung over technology in the Korean company's mobile devices. That Samsung supplies Apple with some of its critical semiconductors for iPhones and iPads seemed to be beside the point.

It's worth considering whether Apple gets away with its behavior because of the rarefied position it enjoys right now, or if there is some universal lesson for other businesses. Certainly Apple has demonstrated that despite its rhetoric, cooperation on one front shouldn't be confused with conflict elsewhere. Apple thinks nothing of viciously attacking its most trusted partners—and then smilingly working with those same partners on other projects. Apple operates by the same rules as the traitorous *capo regime* Salvatore Tessio, in *The Godfather*: "Tell Mike it wasn't personal, just business."

"Frenemies" is one of those annoying Silicon Valley buzzwords that has the virtue of accurately describing life in the technology industry. Oracle once conducted a brutal, personally vindictive, and public campaign against HP over top-level personnel issues even as the two companies continued to integrate their products with each other. Yet Apple operates on a plane of its own: Competitor-partners refrain from angering Apple even as Apple trashes them at will.

There's no escaping that Apple violates—or chooses to ignore—the Golden Rule, *Do unto others as you would have them do unto you.* Is it right for Apple to value its own time more highly than a partner company's? Is it fair for Apple to demand adherence to its brand guidelines while ignoring those of the companies with which it does business? Will a strong dollop of schadenfreude be served up should Apple trip and suddenly look to the kindness of others? The answers seems obvious.

In contrast to the way Apple runs roughshod over its partners and competitors is the subtle way it charms, then entraps its customers—even though they, too, must abide by strict rules in exchange for interacting with Apple. Retail discounts for Apple products don't exist. (Corporate buyers do receive volume discounts, though they say Apple doesn't budge much. Students also catch a small break in Apple stores.) iPhone batteries can't be replaced by their users. New mobile software doesn't work on older versions of the iPod Touch, forcing expensive upgrades to a newer device. And the list goes on.

Little of this dampens the enthusiasm for those who worship at the altar of Apple. "This is not a store," declared retailing expert Paco Underhill, author of the books *Why We Buy What We Buy: The Science of Shopping* and *What Women Want: The Science of Female Shopping.* "It is an exercise in evangelicalism." The temple is a thing of beauty, whether it's in a suburban shopping mall (like the first Apple store, in Tysons Corner, Virginia) or is one of the grand Apple cathedrals on the major boulevards of the world's great cities, including New York's Fifth Avenue, Regent Street in London, and the rue de Rivoli in Paris, across from the Louvre. Visiting an Apple store is like few other retail experiences. Clear, sparse tables hold Apple's products, which are touchable and usable. Up the elegant staircase, often a glass spiral, resides the Genius Bar, a help desk where blue-shirted employees dole out special hand-holding. Elsewhere "sales specialists" hover to answer questions, demonstrate features, and never, ever push for a sale. Why push when customers are so eager to buy?

In fact, Apple has meticulously planned this seemingly effortless shopping experience, going so far as to train its retail employees how to relate to customers and which words to use and which to avoid in dealing with them. "Your job is to understand all of your customers' needs—some of which they may not even realize they have," an Apple training manual states, according to a copy obtained by the *Wall Street Journal*'s Yukari Iwatani Kane and Ian Sherr. The soft sales touch accomplishes the same result as the seemingly organic—but thoroughly planned—corporate marketing message: The customers feel good, but they've been told exactly what Apple wants them to hear.

Apple stores have become a far more visceral "community" meeting place than online networks of friends. From the beginning the company offered targeted, free seminars on how to use Apple technology. Allen Olivo, who ran marketing for Apple's stores when the company started opening them, created a "Made on a Mac" program for experts to talk to users in Apple stores. "We would bring in fashion photographers, and they would sit and talk to three hundred people in LA," he said. "They'd say, 'Here's how I shoot with film or if I shoot digitally, here's how I use Photoshop. Here's how I use my laptop. Here's how it works.' We had disc jockeys from New York City that threw away their turntables and they were using iPods as turntables, and instantly you've got seven hundred people coming into the SoHo store to see their favorite rave deejays talking about how they spin and burn."

Apple continues to host evangelistic and popular events. In late 2011 the children's author Mo Willems spoke at the Apple store on New York's Upper West Side about his new iPad app: "Don't Let the Pigeon Run This App!"

Apple's non-sales sales job seems to be working. The stores generated an average of $43 million in revenue apiece in 2011. This represented revenues of $5,137 per square foot across its stores. In comparison, Best Buy's stores in the US average $850 per square foot, and Tiffany squeezes $3,004 per square foot, according to brokerage firm Sanford Bernstein. In hindsight, it's a wonder anyone ever thought it was a kooky idea for Apple to get into retailing.

Just as Apple didn't invent the music player or the smartphone, it didn't conceive of the specialty store. By the time Apple retail began, Nike, for example, already was operating showcase Nike stores, retail shrines in prime locations like Chicago's North Michigan Avenue, meant to promote the Nike brand as much as to sell sneakers and apparel. Apple wasn't even the first in the computer business to hawk gear at retail. Gateway, the PC maker with the lovable cow prints on its boxes, was operating stores in suburban strip malls even though its primary business was to sell online and by telephone. More prominently, Sony operated select Sony Style stores that were intended to show the elegance of Sony wares while competing minimally with Sony's retail partners.

Apple had broader goals by going into the retail business. It placed its stores in high-traffic locations so it could show off to Windows users; when the stores opened in 2001, that was most of the world. But Apple would most definitely move product. The more product Apple made, in fact, the more valuable its stores became, both as sales venues and as educational opportunities for its customers.

In 2007, Jobs told *Fortune* that the Apple stores had been built to sell the iPhone. He likely was speaking metaphorically—or he was giving a vivid illustration of how far in advance Apple plans its products. The common lore is that Jobs recruited J.Crew CEO Mickey Drexler, then CEO of Gap Inc., to the Apple board to help him craft a retail strategy. In fact, Drexler joined in 1999, before Jobs began hunting for retail executives to run the stores initiative. Apple's march into retail is yet another example of how the company tries to "revolutionize" a familiar concept.

In the case of retail, Apple executives didn't just look at existing stores for inspiration. They asked themselves: *What are the best consumer experiences people have?* Hotels in general—and specifically concierges— came up in response again and again, and the concierge became the inspiration for the Genius Bar. They also talked about what turns people off in stores—clutter, bad design, unfriendly or pushy salespeople. The look of the stores shows Apple's obsession with detail. While each store is distinctive, Apple's architects work with a limited vocabulary of design elements; only three materials, for instance—wood, glass, and steel—are used for store interiors. That's how you know you're in an Apple store regardless of location.

Apple's retail group ultimately helped integrate company offerings in yet another way. Not only did Apple control hardware and software, it also controlled sales. What's more, Apple's stores gave this California-centric company beachheads across the globe. These venues grew into town squares for the good citizens of Appledom. In 2009, when Apple announced it would no longer participate in Macworld—a conference produced by a third-party events-management company, not by Apple—it noted that its participation no longer was necessary. Apple, after all, could communicate directly with its customers in its stores whenever they chose to wander in. In the case of its Fifth Avenue store in New York, it never stopped communicating. That store was open twenty-four hours a day, seven days a week.

Some Apple customers love the company so much that they're taking their affection to a whole new level. In 2010, a few self-described Apple fanboys, one a former Microsoft employee, started Cupidtino, a dating site for Apple product devotees. The Cupidtino.com site is an amusing homage to Apple, and the idea is that people who dig Apple products should somehow dig one another. (The name is a mashup of Cupid and Cupertino.) Fittingly, the look of the site is spare and clean. It uses the Helvetica font, just like Apple does. Icons dance and flip when you click on them, just as they do on Apple.com.

Some thirty-one thousand users have registered for Cupidtino. Its founders say they consciously asked themselves "What would Steve do?" in designing the site. Compared with other dating sites such as Match.com and eHarmony.com, Cupidtino is simple. Instead of long forms, it asks users to fill in four standard descriptions: "What I do," "I became a Mac when...," "Cool facts about me," and "You're my type if..." Cupidtino features a giant photo of each user, which makes sense, given that the user is a well-designed product, a quality item that others should covet. "The emphasis is on what you're getting," said Kintan Brahmbhatt, an adviser to Cupidtino, who happens to be an employee of Amazon.com's IMDb.com division in Seattle. Cupidtino displays photos of prospective dates, he noted, in the same way that Apple displays the iPhone on its website: large and prominent. (The Cupidtino founders know of at least one wedding spawned on their site: a US Marine in Japan named Curtis who found true love by bonding over email with Jesse, a "fangirl" in San Jose who dreamed of working at Apple. The two met when Curtis visited California on leave, and they married a short time later.)

Cupidtino is a labor of love for its founders, yet they're trying to make money at it. Users can send as many messages as they like, but to receive messages, they must subscribe for $4.79 a month, the cost of a twenty-ounce Venti Mocha at a Starbucks in Cupertino. So far, between 2 percent and 5 percent of users pay, said Brahmbhatt, adding that Cupidtino has turned down requests by condom manufacturers and Apple accessories makers to advertise on the site. "We don't want to pollute the site right now," he said. "We want to take a minimalist approach. It's what Steve would have done."

8

Plan for *After* Your Successor

In the days and weeks after Steve Jobs resigned as CEO of Apple on August 24, 2011, there was much handwringing about the future of the company.

The stock price initially fell by a few percentage points. Analysts, reporters, and fanboys tried to parse what little information Jobs disclosed about his being unable to meet his "duties and expectations as Apple's CEO." He died six weeks later.

In his final weeks, Jobs remained as involved in Apple as his strength allowed him to be. Apple executives and board members continued to visit him at his home in Palo Alto. He went out for breakfast and watched a movie at home with his friend Bill Campbell. Little information about his health seeped out, though the website TMZ .com posted a photo of Jobs looking grotesquely gaunt and propped up by a nurse, causing fresh concern among the faithful.

Given all the worry, and the universal consensus that Jobs was the very essence of Apple, a curious thing happened after his resignation. Within less than a month, Apple's stock price hit new all-time highs. The day before his death, the company unveiled a new iPhone, the iPhone 4S, which included an eight-megapixel camera, a faster processor than the iPhone 4, and Siri, the voice-activated personal assistant Jobs had queried at his last board meeting as CEO. When Siri debuted a week after Jobs died, it garnered hugely favorable reviews from critics—David Pogue of the *New York Times* and the *Wall Street Journal*'s Walt Mossberg included. Pre-orders of the new phone topped one million in a single day, surpassing the previous single day pre-order record of six hundred thousand held by its predecessor. Employees, partners, and investors alike had time to prepare for Jobs's passing. He had been in declining health for much of 2011, attending fewer and fewer meetings on the Apple campus. The words he had written in January, when he began his final leave of absence, were prophetic and germane to those considering an Apple without Steve. He said that he had confidence that Tim Cook "and the rest of the executive management team will do a terrific job executing the exciting plans we have in place for 2011." The key word was *executing*, the implication being that Jobs's loyal lieutenants were capably following through on a game plan Jobs already had crafted and approved.

Jobs had done more to ensure that his DNA remain a part of the company than he ever let on publicly. For years, he and other board members had insisted that Apple had a succession plan in place without disclosing what it was. The plan included the obvious manpower issues—who would succeed Jobs as CEO—and also some other measures to make sure that Apple's core values would be passed down to successive generations of leaders.

On the same August day that Jobs relinquished his position as CEO, the board swiftly named Tim Cook the next CEO. Despite rumors that the board had authorized recruiters to shop for another replacement for Jobs, the board never seriously considered naming anyone other than Cook to the position. It was Jobs's board, of course, and he chose Cook, his able sidekick, to take his place.

Jobs thought about far more than who would be the next CEO, however. In the same way that he obsessed on Apple products, he spent years preparing for ways to make sure his vision continues. Starting in 2008, as his health waned and he prepared for a liver transplant, Jobs created a management-training program, but one that was as different from programs that Hewlett-Packard and General Electric had offered as the iPad was from other tablets. Jobs already had some experience with in-house management training. Pixar University offers courses in drawing, painting, sculpting, and filmmaking, as well as leadership. Jobs was thinking beyond vocational skills. He wanted to record, codify, and teach Apple's business history so that its future leaders would have a reference to ensure they thought different. With little fanfare, he created Apple University.

Creating a management-training program seemed at odds with Jobs's "stay hungry, stay foolish" persona—a counterculture persona he had cultivated since reading *The Whole Earth Catalog*. He had long denigrated the value of an MBA. He abhorred the concepts that gave business school professors their jollies, market research chief among them. He generally didn't like MBAs, either.

They had their place, but the people who mattered at an organization like Apple harbored passions for science or art or music, not business. (Forgive Tim Cook, the night school striver who rounded out his credentials while at IBM, his MBA. He's as exceptional in his way as Jobs, the Reed College dropout, was in his.) Pooh-poohing MBAs, though, becomes a problem once a company finds itself one of the largest in the world. It needs structure at that point. It needs leadership. It needs people who think about the business world.

In 2008, Jobs hired Joel Podolny, then the dean of the Yale School of Management, to create Apple University. Podolny, an economic sociologist whose area of expertise is leadership and organizations, was not a typical tweedy academic. He had taught at Stanford and Harvard, but he exhibited very Jobs-like behavior when he became the head of Yale's graduate business school in 2005 at the ripe old age of thirty-nine. Podolny had been a controversial dean during his time in New Haven. He revamped the school's curriculum away from single-topic courses like marketing in favor of topics with wider scopes, like "the employee" and "creativity and innovation." In keeping with Apple's penchant for secrecy and no-profile, Podolny went into a kind of Witness Protection Program when he arrived in Cupertino—especially among his old friends on the Stanford faculty. "He has become, how shall I put it, super clammed up about Apple," said Hayagreeva "Huggy" Rao, a Stanford business professor, who, like others among the Stanford faculty, said he didn't see much of Podolny. Initially hired to create Apple University, Podolny later was promoted to vice president of human resources, despite never having run an HR department.

Jobs himself had long ignored the HR function at Apple, choosing to focus primarily on recruiting, which he considered critical. He was attuned to the fact, however, that Apple was missing out by shunning general management and avoiding leaders with traditional business backgrounds. "We don't hire a lot of MBAs, but we believe in teaching and learning," he once said. "We do want to create our own MBA, but in our image. We've got more interesting cases than anyone."

Podolny hired a handful of additional professors such as Harvard's Richard Tedlow, and they began writing cases about Apple. Tedlow, who is sixty-four, is the preeminent US academic business historian and is best known for chronicling the lives and careers of the most successful American entrepreneurs of modern times, including George Eastman, Henry Ford, and Thomas Watson. He took a leave of absence from Harvard, where he was the MBA Class of 1949 Professor of Business Administration, to consult at Apple. Then, in 2011—and without so much as a press release—he retired from Harvard after twenty-three years to take up a full-time position at Apple. "He told me he's doing what he did here but that he's doing it for internal Apple executives," said Richard Vietor, a Harvard colleague.

Examples of the case studies being taught at Apple University include the story of how Apple crafted its retail strategy from scratch and Apple's approach to commissioning factories in China. Wherever possible the cases shine a light on mishaps, the thinking being that a company has the most to learn from its mistakes. Apple executives teach the cases, with guidance from the professors.

In his own book *Giants of Enterprise*, Tedlow makes

trenchant observations about the challenges great companies face:

> There is no other field of human activity—including entertainment, sports, high fashion, or politics—which is so riddled by fads as business. Every day there is a newspaper headline, every week there is a magazine story, and perhaps with the Internet we will soon be saying every hour there is yet another "guru" that touts a new hero of business or a new method of solving problems which date back not merely ten years but far longer. At the least, the study of business history can prompt an executive to ask of each new "solution" to problems that can never be solved but only managed: How really lasting is this approach, this idea, this company?

Drawing comparisons among the visionaries he researched, Tedlow observes that the men who created these great enterprises suffered from "the derangement of power." He notes, "It is very common among the very powerful and very destructive. Norwegians have, in fact, a word for this syndrome. It is *stormannsgalskap*, which can be translated as 'great men's madness.'" If any company could fairly be described as being influenced by a leader with *stormannsgalskap*, it was Apple.

If Tedlow has been addressing the subject of great men's madness with his students, word hasn't yet leaked out. Instead, he is teaching them business lessons about other companies that the Apple executives can apply to their own situations. For instance, Tedlow has lectured Apple's PR staff on the Tylenol tampering crisis of 1982 and how the McNeil Consumer Products unit of Johnson & Johnson responded. He taught a class for executives about the fallen grocery store chain A&P as an example of what happened to a company that once dominated its field. Quipped an attendee: "We were all trying to figure out what A&P had to do with Apple."

Apple spent years keeping academics out, so it will be interesting to see over time the effect of welcoming them in. Tedlow's last book before joining Apple was *Denial: Why Business Leaders Fail to Look Facts in the Face—and What to Do About It*. Marketing material for the book notes that a common sign of denial is the act of "focusing on a glitzy new headquarters rather than the competition." Apple hardly ignores the competition. Then again, the last time he spoke in public, on June 7, 2011, Jobs unveiled plans for a magnificent new Apple headquarters, which he likened to a giant spaceship.

The effect of Apple University on the company's corporate culture could take years to become visible to outsiders. Some of the first perceptible differences between the Jobs and the post-Jobs eras will be seen sooner—in areas that were outside Jobs's interest, or areas where the company's shortcomings were directly attributable to him. Apple hardly was a perfect place under Jobs, so while his death represents a great loss, it also presents an opportunity. For example, a dirty little secret inside Apple is that Jobs was a one-man bottleneck. Steve Jobs was all too human, after all, and there was only so much he could do in the course of a day. Employees liked to say there were two kinds of projects at Apple: the ones Steve Jobs obsessed over and all the others. In fact, Apple tends to be a one-big-thing-at-a-time company, reflecting the legendary CEO's willingness to concentrate only on one big thing at a time.

When Jobs was CEO, a former Apple engineer described this phenomenon in predictably computer-scientist lingo: "He operates in a single-threaded manner. Other things will get put on hold." When the first iPhone was under development, for example, the scheduled update of the operating system for the Macintosh was delayed by months because of the resources pulled to focus on the first mobile operating system.

Jobs's refusal to spread himself too thin at Apple—a problem alleviated only somewhat when he sold Pixar to Disney in 2006 and stopped spending a day a week at the animated film company across the San Francisco Bay—was consistent with how he wanted Apple to run. Generally speaking, Apple doesn't multitask. The lower down employees are in the ranks, the more they focus on one project. The virtues of this approach are evident in Apple's exceptional and limited product lineup. But having a singularity of focus has downsides, too. Apple is a sprawling, multiproduct company now. There's reason to believe that less visionary managers will be willing to keep more balls in the air—at a time when Apple already is juggling more balls.

Another little-discussed topic at Apple, given its success, is what could be called its orphan products, the features that Apple plainly doesn't care all that much about. During Jobs's tenure, employees knew the reason when one of their projects seemed to simmer on the back burner: Jobs wasn't interested. An example is the inferiority of Apple's spreadsheet program, Numbers, compared with its stellar presentation software, Keynote. "Keynote is a wonderful application because Steve did presentations," a departed engineer pointed out. "Numbers doesn't ooze *Steveness*, which makes sense, because Steve didn't do spreadsheets." Indeed, in the context of extolling the virtues of having one person, the CFO, keep a spreadsheet for the company's finances, Jobs once boasted: "Nobody walks around with spreadsheets anymore." It's a ludicrous statement, of course. Tim Cook is a master of spreadsheets, and there's no way a legion of Apple managers working on projects from real estate to logistics to manufacturing could function without them. But the sentiment nevertheless reflected Jobs's attitude, and in fact Numbers isn't a real rival to Microsoft's Excel. If Apple wanted to make a serious effort to court business users for its computers, creating a better spreadsheet program would be a step in the right direction.

Whole sectors of the company were ignored when something else had caught Jobs's fancy, and they typically were slower-growing units. Macintosh computers faced this fate, for instance. Employees are completely aware of the phenomenon, and many who leave the company cite having found themselves in an un-hot corner of Apple with no opportunity to move.

A new regime at Apple may institute subtler and more salubrious changes. Technology wonks like to gripe that Apple's products *look* more beautiful than they are. In other words, Apple is accused of sacrificing mechanical design for industrial design. It's a debatable point, as these same critics typically will say that Apple's less-than-perfect products are still better than anyone else's. Fair or not, Apple's emphasis on aesthetics over functionality is directly attributable to the leadership of Steve Jobs. If there is room for improvement here, his absence may provide the opening.

A post-Jobs Apple also may enter the modern era of financial management. Jobs for years was insistent that Apple maintain a strong balance sheet, so fearful was he of reliving the late-1990s experience of nearly going broke. He loathed stock buybacks, arguing, with good reason, that they are bribes to investors rather than good uses of capital. Keeping more than $75 billion lying around is nobody's idea of good financial management, however. And Wall Street types have all sorts of suggestions for how Apple could do better here, such as paying dividends or investing the cash more aggressively. Such topics were considered off the table with Jobs. He treated cash as if he had lived through the Great Depression. What investors would view as modern balance-sheet management would have to wait for a CEO with an MBA. Tim Cook has an MBA, and he speaks regularly to investors, which is a start.

There's also the hint of evidence Apple can become a kinder, gentler place in the post-Jobs era. One of Tim Cook's first official acts was to offer a corporate philanthropic matching program for employees. Jobs was notoriously stingy when it came to giving away money. He argued privately that the most philanthropic action Apple could take was to increase the value of the company so shareholders could give away their wealth to the causes of their choice, not Apple's. Given his politically liberal leanings, Jobs reasoned that investors would prefer things that way. (Laurene Powell Jobs was even further to the left of her husband. Jobs joked to his biographer, Walter Isaacson, that he needed to "hide the knives" before inviting the right-wing News Corp. chairman Rupert Murdoch over for dinner.)

Nevertheless, two weeks after becoming CEO, Cook told Apple's US employees that the company would match gifts to charities up to $10,000 annually. "Thank you all for working so hard to make a difference, both here at Apple and in the lives of others," Cook wrote in a companywide email. "I am incredibly proud to be part of this team."

Philanthropy and a spreadsheet program to compete with Microsoft are just some of the tea leaves that optimists about Apple's future bring up when they talk about the company after Jobs. Certain quirks will be ironed out for the better without him, they say.

There is a pessimistic view, too, that Apple will become less dynamic, its products less coveted, without Jobs. The glass-is-half-empty crowd envisions a scenario in which the pipeline of devices that we don't even know we want yet runs dry in a few years. "Apple designed for Steve," a former Apple software engineer said. "It is not an exaggeration. Steve was the user that everything orbited around and was designed for."

The entrepreneur Mike McCue, who never worked at Apple but is one of those start-up junkies who long idolized Jobs, tells a story that illustrates the Steve-as-linchpin perspective. "I once spoke with Jony Ive about how wonderfully connected Apple's whole product line was," McCue said.

I was standing in an Apple store, back when they came out with their first set of new Macs and OS X [Apple's desktop software]. And I remember looking up at the screen, and their website had these sort of

gray translucent lines thematically in the website. And
if you ran your eye up the screen, up to the menu bar
of OS X it had these gray translucent lines. And then
you ran your eye up even further in the cinema display and they had these gray translucent lines. And
then I looked over to my left and there was a barrier,
a glass barrier that separated [the different areas of
the store] and it had these gray translucent lines. And
I asked Jony, "How did that happen? Who does that
at Apple?" And he was like, "Steve does that."

Jobs also dominated Apple in an intangible way. He
was the final arbiter on matters of taste. A former Apple
engineer who left for a Silicon Valley start-up described
the differences in how math-oriented Google and design-
oriented Apple work. When Jobs was CEO, he made
decisions on matters as routine as the color palette for a
website. "Let's say Google is trying to determine the correct color for a new page," said the engineer. "It will order
an analytical test by serving up various shades of blue to
one million Google.com users and then analyze the click-
through rates." Google, in other words, takes a democratic
approach: Users can't be wrong, and they vote with their
clicks. What's more, were an engineer even to have an
opinion about the correct shade of blue, he'd be outvoted
by the user analysis. At Google, crowdsourcing rules.

User democracy is the antithesis of how Apple operates. Jobs famously told customers what they wanted.
He didn't ask their opinion. "The Apple way is that Steve
picked the color he liked and that's the color," the former
Apple engineer concluded. "He was willing to listen to
counterarguments. But if you [were] arguing taste or opin-

ion, it was a losing battle." This view of Apple as a kind of consumer-electronics fashion house leaves little hope for a new creative and entrepreneurial genius to rise from the ranks. After all, with Jobs calling the shots on matters of style across the company, his subordinates won't have been able to try their hands at the game.

Finally, there is a third view—the grand hope of Apple's supporters, the optimistic viewpoint—that Steve Jobs so thoroughly stamped the company with his DNA, the fledglings are ready to fly on their own. Therapist/ business coach Michael Maccoby, the expert on visionary and narcissistic leaders, identified indoctrination as one of the productive narcissist's primary goals.

> The narcissistic CEO wants all his subordinates to think the way he does about the business. Productive narcissists—people who often have a dash of the obsessive personality—are good at converting people to their point of view...[Jack] Welch's strategy has been extremely effective. GE managers must either internalize his vision, or they must leave. Clearly, this is incentive learning with a vengeance. I would even go so far as to call Welch's teaching brainwashing. But Welch does have the rare insight and know-how to achieve what all narcissistic business leaders are trying to do—namely, *get the organization to identify with them, to think the way they do, and to become the living embodiment of their companies.* [Emphasis added.]

As I've noted, legend has it that in the years following Walt Disney's death in 1966, top Disney executives were known to ask, "What would Walt do?" But the Walt Disney Company is a cautionary tale for students of Apple because Disney declined precipitously when Walt was gone. In the years after Disney died, his lieutenants pumped out a final volley of classic old-school Disney animated musicals—Walt's pipeline of products. *The Jungle Book* in 1967 was one. But then the output got spotty and weird (*The Black Cauldron, The Great Mouse Detective*). It really wasn't until 1988, with *Who Framed Roger Rabbit?*, and *The Little Mermaid* the following year, that Disney's animation efforts got back on track. These films triggered the Disney renaissance, but there were a lot of elements in both of them Walt might not have approved of. The voluptuous Jessica Rabbit comes to mind as well as the sea witch, Ursula, whose body was based on the drag queen and John Waters staple Divine.

Even with these successes, under the leadership of an executive hired from Paramount, Michael Eisner, Disney fell so far behind on innovation that it had to buy Pixar. That company, funded by Steve Jobs, did see the future of computer-aided animation, forcing Disney to play catch-up on the latest technology in a field Disney invented.

The question Apple faces is whether or not Steve Jobs's view of the world has been imprinted enough on the top leadership of Apple that they can carry on without him, but on their own authority, not his. "The first and second rungs of Apple management were exposed to him for a long time," said one former Apple executive, who continues to monitor the company closely. "Through a process of forceful osmosis they have gotten good at channeling him."

This hopeful notion holds that the top executives at Apple, and the single layer of managers beneath them, have become so good at their discrete jobs that they'll know exactly what to do in the future. Before Jobs died, Apple engineers would end debates by invoking a threat along the lines of: *Do you want to be the one to tell Steve that can't be done?* Keeping such auto-editing going will be possible for some length of time. Jony Ive presumably already told Jobs as much about design as Jobs told Ive— and can be counted on to be Apple's tastemaker going forward. Apple managers and their employees alike have been trained to execute their tasks—and will remain under tremendous pressure not to disappoint their colleagues. "There is so little ambiguity at Apple," said a former Apple marketing executive. "The wind is going to blow in that sail for a long time."

For all the fears of Apple's demise without Steve Jobs, there is also the assertion that Apple likely will stand above the crowd for some time to come, partly because of its own excellence, but also because of the limitations of the crowd. Avie Tevanian, the longtime senior Apple software executive who left the company in 2006, said a few weeks before Jobs died: "When Steve is gone, the competition still will not have Steve Jobs."

Steve Jobs was an entrepreneur, and the task of an entrepreneur is to start companies that will kill off existing leaders. So in a way Jobs had started thinking about the causes of corporate death at an unusually young age. He understood that one of the biggest challenges facing established companies—and people, for that matter—was

stagnation. "Human minds settle into fixed ways of looking at the world, and that's always been true," he said
in a 1995 interview for the Smithsonian Institution's oral
history project. "I've always felt that death is the greatest
invention of life. I'm sure that life evolved without death
at first and found that without death, life didn't work very
well because it didn't make room for the young." At the
time of the interview Jobs was trying to build NeXT, a
software company aiming to disrupt existing players. He
also was at the precipice of success with Pixar, a tiny company that was out-innovating the giant Disney.

He clearly had the failure of Apple on his mind, though,
as he reflected on the problem with big companies.

> One of the things that happens in organizations
> as well as with people is that they settle into ways
> of looking at the world and become satisfied with
> things. And the world changes and keeps evolv-
> ing and new potential arises, but these people who
> are settled in don't see it. That's what gives start-up
> companies their greatest advantage. The seden-
> tary point of view is that of most large companies.
> In addition to that, large companies do not usually
> have efficient communication paths from the peo-
> ple closest to some of these changes at the bottom
> of the company to the top of the company which
> are the people making the big decisions...Even
> in the case where part of the company does the
> right thing at the lower levels, usually the upper
> levels screw it up somehow. I mean IBM and the
> personal computer business is a good example
> of that. I think as long as humans don't solve this

human nature trait of sort of settling into a world-view after a while, there will always be opportunity for young companies; young people to innovate, as it should be.

The words are prophetic, given how far Apple traveled after Jobs said them. They're also instructive, both as a way of understanding the mind-set and culture Jobs instilled at Apple and also as food for thought for the many big companies that suffer from exactly the maladies Jobs described. Days before Meg Whitman was named chief executive of Hewlett-Packard in September 2011, she mused to the *Wall Street Journal* about the difficulty big companies have keeping up with rapid change. "The bigger you get, the harder it is to be nimble. How do you grow big and stay small? That still is the fundamental question."

Maybe for Meg Whitman and HP. But growing big while feeling like a start-up was Apple's preoccupation for fifteen years. Culturally, Apple demonstrated a start-up's willingness to try new things by moving into the music and video industries. It corrected an earlier mistake of not being open to third-party developers by creating its App Store. Importantly, the App Store was not Apple's first instinct. It opened eight months after the iPhone was released. But Apple saw that Google intended to create an applications store with its Android environment and also that developers were enthusiastically creating illegal "hacks" on the iPhone in order to run their unauthorized programs, often video games. Apple reacted quickly and forcefully, admitting a mistake without ever saying so.

Apple insiders say it is preposterous to literally think of

Apple as a start-up. There are too many rules, too many people, too little freedom for that to be the case. What Jobs figured out, however, was how to create the effect of a start-up within a giant organization when and where it was warranted. Thus Jonathan Ive's industrial design team operates like a tiny consultancy, albeit one with massive resources and a direct line to the client. Developers on special projects are hived off in a stealthy zone that gives the illusion of being a start-up. All the while, more mature parts of Apple operate like any big company: slower growth, iteration of its products rather than wholesale redesigns, difficulty getting the attention of senior management, and so on.

Over the next fifteen years or so, the business world will get to watch the drama of whether Apple truly has found a way to cheat the hangman's noose or if the period between 1997 and 2012 or so was a golden aberration driven by one extraordinary individual the likes of which we'll never see again. If the former is true, then Apple will defy almost all of business history.

Geoffrey West, the Santa Fe Institute physicist, studies the life span of organizations. His groundbreaking research showed that cities, with few exceptions, never die. More recently he, together with colleagues Luis Bettencourt and Marcus Hamilton, has turned his attention to companies, studying a data set of more than twenty thousand publicly listed outfits. West's conclusion: The exact opposite is true for companies, which not only tend to die, but behave like living organisms.

"We studied scaling laws and asked: How do organisms change when you change the size of the organism?" said West, whose unruly white beard and devil-may-care demeanor make him a cross between Old Saint Nick and the mad scientist from Central Casting. "People, which are organisms, are stable for a long time. They grow for fifteen or sixteen years, then live for another fifty stably." His conclusion was that companies bear an uncanny resemblance to humans. "Companies generically all have a kind of sigmoidal growth curve of a living organism." (A sigmoidal curve grows quickly, plateaus for a time, and then declines.) "Almost all of biology is like that. The same data led to our discovery that companies die."

The similarities between Jobs's fifteen-year-old musings and West's scientific conclusions are striking. West continues:

A company begins as a start-up. It creates tremendous buzz and goes through a period where anything goes. There is no concern for paying bills as the company explores new rules. Below a level of fifty employees, there seems to be a lot of random behavior. Between fifty and one hundred employees, if the company has survived, this is when the sigmoidal behavior begins. At that stage the company needs bureaucracy, human resources, compliance, and so on. The company more and more becomes the bureaucracy. The innovative phase gets phased out, unlike a city. A city tolerates all sorts of crazy people walking around. No corporation will tolerate that. Companies become very intolerant to new ideas, rhetoric to the contrary. When a company starts cutting down the bloat, it no longer can be cool. The last time I was at Google I already could feel the tentacles of the bureaucracy encroaching—and Google's awareness of the problem. There are signs of mortality creeping in. It may well be that Apple recognizes this problem and is fighting it like crazy by being open to new ideas. The question is: Is that possible?

Apple already has survived several transformations. It endured the transition from tiny start-up to bloated multinational. Then it slimmed down to essentially a single-product company before beginning again to broaden its product line.

With all the attention focused on the death of Steve Jobs, it has been less noticed that an even more significant—and, internally anyway, unsettling—shift was under way. In 2001, shortly after Apple introduced the iPod and its retail stores, desktop and notebook computers made up the bulk of Apple's business. In 2011, iPhones accounted for 44 percent of Apple's revenues, iPads made up 19 percent, and iPods another 7 percent. All desktop and notebook computers amounted to 20 percent of the overall pie.

Culturally, this represents a massive change. "I was there when [the transition] was mid-swing," reflected Frederick Van Johnson, product marketing manager from 2002 to 2005. "Initially, it was all about the Mac. iLife was created to sell Macs. That was the point. The whole building was about selling more Macs. It started swinging with iTunes. People said, 'Oh crap, we're making more money selling bits than we are atoms.'" Now a similar swing is in motion with the shift to non-PC devices and "cloud" services like iCloud, a radical shift for the industry and for Apple. "It's becoming a completely different company," said Johnson. "It has left people in a kind of kerfuffle.

They're afraid. You've been working on the cruise ship and your job has been selling drinks, and now the cruise ship is changing to something else. Now it's a cargo liner: What's your job? Are they going to find a place for you?"

Apple is a company of paradoxes. Its people and institutional bearing are off-the-charts arrogant, yet at the same time they are genuinely fearful of what would happen if their big bets go bad. The creative side of the business that was dominated by Steve Jobs is made up of lifers or near lifers who value only an Apple way of doing things—hardly the typical creative mind-set. The operations side of Apple runs like any company in America, but better, and is led by a cadre of ex-IBMers, the cultural antithesis of Apple. Apple has an entrepreneurial flair yet keeps its people in a tightly controlled box, following time-tested procedures. Its public image, at least seen through its advertising, is whimsical and fun, yet its internal demeanor is cheerless and nose-to-the-grindstone.

Tim Cook undoubtedly is mindful of his own weaknesses and the hole that Steve Jobs left. There's no way he'll aim to remake Apple in his own image. The trick will be finding the right leaders who can guide Apple in a way that Steve Jobs would have appreciated, understanding that it's impossible—and even foolhardy—to try to run the company the way Jobs would have. In this regard, Tim Cook may be a caretaker CEO of Apple, even if his regency lasts ten years.

9

Inspire Imitators

An unexpected guest crashed Tony Fadell's first date with the woman who would become his wife. Fadell joined Apple in 2001 as part of a special products group, ultimately becoming senior vice president of the iPod division. Danielle Lambert was a top recruiting executive who later became Apple's VP of human resources. Fadell had been at the company for about a year when a co-worker set him up with Lambert. The two met for their blind date in the lobby of 1 Infinite Loop, where, rather than leaving for dinner or a drink, they sat for hours talking.

In the middle of their love-at-first-sight moment, Steve Jobs appeared. He walked up to the budding couple and started a conversation with Lambert, ignoring Fadell, who assumed it was the CEO's way of showing his disapproval. After a twelve-week, highly hush-hush courtship, the two became engaged, but they immediately told Jobs. He called them into his office and said, "I have always been advised: Never allow anyone at the company to be married to anyone who is senior in HR." Fadell said Jobs agreed to make an exception for them. But he had a warning. "I trust you will keep your professional life separate and never discuss anything about work," Jobs said.

Fadell and Lambert married and continued working at Apple for most of the decade. Fadell became one of Apple's most celebrated executives, called the "father of the iPod" in the press and whispered about as a future Apple CEO. He left Apple, however, in 2008, after clashing repeatedly with Jobs as well as with his software counterpart, Scott Forstall. Jobs valued Fadell so much that despite banishing him from Apple's executive team, he kept Fadell on as an adviser to the CEO for a little over a year. ("Advisers" often are paid so they won't "advise" anyone else; Fadell received an annual salary of $300,000 and shares worth more than $8 million not to work for an Apple competitor.)

Since ending his relationship with Apple, Fadell began a high-stakes experiment: testing the hypothesis that Apple executives can translate their skills outside Infinite Loop. Top Apple people have left to join other companies, but most don't. Fadell is the first member of the modern Apple executive team to start a consumer-electronics company from scratch. Given his triumphs at Apple, his success or failure will speak volumes to how well the Apple experience translates.

Fadell's new company, Nest, doesn't compete with Apple. Not yet anyway. It markets a "learning thermostat," a $249 device that mildly competent do-it-yourselfers can install to replace the dumb thermostat in their homes. Nest's device is intelligent. (Fadell calls it a "smartphone with some temperature controls.") It learns a user's desired behavior and adjusts the environment according to whether someone is home or away, among other energy-saving tricks. The device wouldn't look out of place at an Apple store, with its smooth chrome circular design housing an LED screen. Though he didn't work in product marketing at Apple, Fadell has mastered the keep-it-simple technique for describing a new product. The three key facets of the Nest thermostat verily trip off his tongue: "It saves energy, it programs itself, and it's beautiful."

Fadell worked at other companies before Apple, including Philips Electronics and the now defunct General Magic, itself a popular repository of Apple alumni from an earlier generation. This gives him perspective on what he'll take from his Apple experience and what he won't—or, in some cases, can't. "Even if you have constrained resources, do not cut corners," said Fadell, stating his number one rule from Apple. "People will feel it." He noted that Nest spends far more than a typical start-up. For example, it includes a custom-designed screwdriver with each thermostat—a bit of customer hand-holding meant to ease the pain of installation. "Our ops guys are like, 'Get rid of it,'" said Fadell, citing their argument that customers already have screwdrivers and the unnecessary expense will hurt margins. Fadell defends the screwdriver for its contribution to user experience. On the flip side, Nest by necessity is a humbler company than Apple. He likened it to the Apple of 2001 and 2002, "when we were trying to prove we had something of value" with the iPod. Nest must outsource customer service, unlike Apple. "We also don't have Apple's leverage with Best Buy," said Fadell. "It's more of a shared relationship."

If Tony Fadell had risen up the ranks at General Electric rather than Apple, it's likely he'd be running a major corporation today. There was a moment during the end of the Jack Welch era when GE was viewed as the incubator for CEOs. Boeing, Home Depot, Honeywell, Albertsons, and Nielsen were just some of the companies that plucked GE executives to run them. The company's unique management mojo convinced many boards that if executives could thrive in the Land of Six Sigma, they could do anything. So pervasive was GE's legendary stature that Tina Fey could wring multiple seasons of guffaws on the TV show *30 Rock* from the relentless ambition and management bromides of Jack Donaghy, GE's fictional Vice President of East Coast Television and Microwave Oven Programming.

Judging whether the Apple way is a portable system is trickier for a couple of reasons. Apple's senior executives tend to stick around a long time and often are exhausted— and very wealthy—when they're done. Apple hasn't until very recently begun to train managers in any formal way. Much of the learning has been by osmosis, and even so, huge swaths of relatively senior executives aren't exposed to something as basic as a financial analysis. For many years, it was rare to see an ex–Apple executive reappearing in a leadership role at another tech company compared with the number of former Oracle executives, for example, who have gone on to run billion-dollar enterprises including Salesforce.com, PeopleSoft, Siebel Systems, Veritas, and Informatica.

The data set of Apple alumni leaving Cupertino and trying their hands elsewhere, in other words, is small. But a few have taken up significant roles, typically after a post-Apple grace period. Mitch Mandich, who ran sales at Apple following the NeXT acquisition, later founded a high-profile ethanol company called Range Fuels that struggled to gain traction.

Jon Rubinstein ran hardware engineering at Apple, including the division that made the first iPod. After leaving Apple, he became CEO of Palm in a turnaround effort. Rubinstein completely revamped Palm's smartphone lineup, to critical acclaim. But Palm failed to take hold in the market as an independent company—a victim of having too little money to go toe-to-toe with Apple and Google in the fast-growing smartphone market. (A secret of success for Apple's new products and Google's Android mobile operating system is that their efforts are funded lavishly by existing cash-cow products, the Mac in Apple's case and search advertising for Google. Palm had no such advantages.)

Fred Anderson, Apple's longtime chief financial officer, helped found the private-equity firm Elevation Partners, which blundered with ill-timed investments, including Palm. Elevation counted another friend of Apple, and Steve Jobs, among its partners: U2 front man Bono. Awkwardly for Elevation and Palm, and Apple for that matter, U2 became spokesmodels for Research in Motion's Black-Berry smartphone.

Going forward, the business world will get to watch a top Apple executive try to apply his considerable success at Apple to another company. In late 2011, retail chief Ron Johnson became the CEO of JCPenney, vowing to turn around the retailer by reinventing the department store. Johnson's reputation reached heroic proportions at Apple. A former VP of merchandising at Target who led the team responsible for launching Michael Graves's exclusive line of products, Johnson was the founding head of Apple's retail stores. Having taken the Apple retail concept global—by the end of Apple's fiscal year in 2011 the company had 357 stores in eleven countries—Johnson was ready for a change.

For years it was an article of faith in Silicon Valley that Apple should not be emulated. Its closed approach to business as well as to hardware and software development was widely deemed to have been a grievous strategic error, allowing a technologically inferior Microsoft to dominate the industry. Even after the success of the last ten-plus years, remarkably few big companies openly mimic Apple. HP, for example, is experimenting with retail stores in Latin America and Canada, but not in the United States. The Apple approach seems to hold more sway among the younger generation of entrepreneurs, especially in Silicon Valley. These Tech 2.0 titans admire Apple's obsession with detail and the company's ability to build a closed world that seduces and ensnares consumers.

Elon Musk, for example, a founder of PayPal as well as the space-exploration start-up SpaceX, paid homage to Apple by hiring one of its top retail executives, George Blankenship, to oversee the nascent sales efforts of Tesla Motors, Musk's fledgling electric-car venture. Blankenship, who worked at the Gap for the first twenty years of his career, is vice president for "worldwide sales and ownership experience" for Tesla. What "sales and ownership experience" means to a new company like Tesla is the location and design of its retail showrooms, as distinctly different from a traditional auto dealership as Apple's retail boutiques were from a big-box Circuit City store.

Blankenship, a trim, goateed fifty-eight-year-old, is ideally suited for the Tesla assignment. He ran real estate operations for Gap, the multibrand retailing behemoth, and then signed on with Apple in 2000 to be its site-selection guru for the nascent Apple stores. "I sit here today and look at Tesla, and I see Apple ten or eleven years ago, when I joined," he said. As we chatted, we were sitting in a lounge area of the Tesla "showroom" in San Jose. Tesla showrooms aren't dealerships—a legal distinction in certain states. But they're also not meant to evoke the dealership vibe. Salesmen with short-sleeved dress shirts and ugly ties are nowhere to be found on the premises. Tesla's site selection itself is unusual: The San Jose showroom sits in the middle of the high-end Santana Row shopping center, located between BCBG Max Azria and Franco Uomo clothing stores. It is nowhere near a freeway off-ramp. The walls are painted in an arresting dark red, with giant Apple monitors displaying Tesla promotional videos. An interactive touch screen on one wall allows prospective car buyers to design the interior of their dream electric car.

His mission at Tesla, said Blankenship, is the same as Apple's goal was back when its stores opened: get uninformed customers familiar with a new product they otherwise wouldn't have been inclined to even consider. "I sort of look at the iPod as a big step forward for Apple because up until then it was trying to build confidence and get people comfortable coming into the store," he said. "And then comes the iPod. It cost $400. Most of the music players at that time were $149. What's the difference? Well, the difference is this one is 'a thousand songs in your pocket.'" Whether or not other players held a thousand songs was beside the point. Apple came up with the easily repeatable marketing line that perfectly captured the iPod's capability. Blankenship described Tesla's version, an obvious homage to Apple marketing, regarding how to sell its $150,000-plus Roadster. "Zero to sixty in 3.7 seconds," he said. "Well, that's impossible. Nope. Get in the car and ride it and you'll see, it's zero to sixty in 3.7 seconds. Two hundred forty-five miles on a charge. That's impossible. Nope, not in our cars. So what happens is you begin developing a customer who wants your car. It's not about price, it's about wanting the car."

The comparisons between Apple and Tesla don't stop with the stores or the marketing message for its first, expensive product. Just as Apple followed the original iPod with a far less pricey iPod Mini, Tesla plans to unveil a $57,000 sedan called the Model S. "We have people waiting in line to be able to buy a Model S, because they want the car," he said, not needing to add that many of these people admired but couldn't necessarily afford the Roadster. (Celebrity owners such as actors George Clooney and Dustin Hoffman and superagent Ari Emanuel clearly could afford one.)

Blankenship is hard-pressed to find any differences between how Apple approached retail and how Tesla hopes to sell cars: "They were trying to get into the buying decision, we're in the buying decision. They were trying to overcome a preconceived idea. We're trying to overcome a new technology that we're trying to introduce. They didn't want to focus on price. We're not focused on price. They wanted to have a great experience. We want to have a great experience."

There's one thing at Apple Tesla doesn't plan to emulate

just yet. "Elon actually asked me...'Do you think we should do a Top 100?' I said, 'Not yet. There's really no need for that yet.'" Apple, Blankenship explained, was broadening its portfolio from computers to music to phones. Such things called for senior-level coordination. Tesla, for the time being, sells one model.

Tesla executives admire Apple's messaging and approach to retail, while other entrepreneurs at Web 2.0 companies including Facebook, Twitter, and Inkling have studied Apple in the hope of appropriating other elements of its success. Whereas Apple was barely part of the conversation a decade ago, especially among Internet companies, today it is Topic A. "We look at Apple as an extraordinary model," said Sheryl Sandberg, the chief operating officer of Facebook and a veteran of Google. "We study its approach to everything from the consistency of its messaging to how it structures its business."

Facebook has created a "closed" (that is, non-Web-based) platform while encouraging others to build applications within Facebook, on Facebook's terms. (Sound familiar?) Facebook's young founder and CEO, Mark Zuckerberg, frequently walked in Palo Alto with Steve Jobs, seeking the older man's advice. Sandberg, who served on the Disney board with Jobs, said the Apple example also is valuable for managing her relationship with Zuckerberg. "I work for a founder-driven company," she said. "Seeing how Jobs channeled his passion and intensity helped me appreciate how I can help Mark realize his vision for Facebook."

One acclaimed Silicon Valley entrepreneur is said to

have been so enamored with Jobs that he is modeling himself after him. Jack Dorsey, the inventor of Twitter, emulated Jobs by taking on an operating role at Twitter while also serving as CEO of Square, a mobile-payments processing start-up he founded. (Jobs gave less of his time to Pixar but was heavily involved, for instance, in Pixar's sale to Disney while he was CEO of Apple.) Square's elegant white credit card reader easily could be mistaken for having come out of Apple's industrial design lab.

Meanwhile, a handful of former Apple employees are starting their own companies, taking with them the lessons they learned at Apple. "Culture is the sum of things that we encourage and discourage," said Matt MacInnis, a former Apple education marketing executive who founded a digital publishing company called Inkling that initially produced textbooks solely for the iPad. MacInnis listed some of Inkling's founding values, all borrowed from his experiences at Apple: "Don't talk about product until it's done. Have high expectations. Don't talk about the road map with the entire company."

Even entrepreneurs who had success before Apple's resurgence are studying its ways. Mike McCue was a young executive at Netscape and later founded Tellme Networks, which he sold to Microsoft for nearly $1 billion. His latest start-up is Flipboard, a publishing platform that aims to upend the magazine industry by aggregating content on the iPad. McCue said he's been studying Apple since its earliest days. As an entrepreneur, he embraces Apple's notion of "building technology not for technology's sake, but to change the world, to make a 'dent in the universe,' as they used to say." He overtly thinks about the simplicity of Apple's design and attention to detail. "We are primarily about building a really pure user experience that is heavily thought through," said McCue. "We will spend hours and hours and hours talking about a 'close' button in the corner of the screen and mocking it up, and going through hundreds of different design iterations on that before we settle on one that we like. That kind of attention to detail means that as a result you really can't do a lot of things. You have to just do a few things really, really well."

Not every company and not every executive will be able to copy Apple. Some companies are too complicated for one P&L. (It's conceivable Apple may one day also be too complicated for one P&L.) Some industries demand market research. An oil giant, for example, is not going to drill for oil without first forming an opinion about demand.

But it's hard to imagine that the basic tenets of the Apple way can't be imitated. Who would argue for not focusing, or for not holding employees accountable? What maker of products or deliverer of services wouldn't benefit from asking the question: Are we basing that decision on what's best for the product, and therefore for the customer? Is there a company that couldn't benefit from a critical examination of its messaging, to at least ask the questions: Are we simplifying the message enough? Is our point clear? How many companies allow their PR departments to serve multiple masters and purposes, including CEO ego gratification, as opposed to pushing product? Is there something to consider in discouraging employees from being distracted by pursuits that may help them but not the company? Is career development always best for the shareholders?

As an unabashed admirer of start-ups, Jobs fought like crazy to have Apple retain some of a start-up's characteristics. In fact, though medium-sized and large companies will want to study Apple's ways, its best lessons may be for start-ups. Because Apple was so sick when Jobs returned, he was able to treat it as a reboot, what the rest of the world would call a turnaround project. Yet the Apple of the late 1990s was very much an upstart. It had little to lose and everything to gain from casting aside the industry's ways of doing things. The management and operational characteristics of the reborn Apple are a treasure trove of guideposts for all business; they are a veritable handbook for entrepreneurs.

The biggest pitfall in trying to be like Apple, however, is that Apple's culture is thirty-five years in the making and bears the stamp of one extraordinary entrepreneur who turned into a shrewd chief executive of a sixty-thousand-person corporation. It won't be a snap for any company to create its own version of the Apple culture. As well, Apple itself will find out how strong its culture really is—and how much of its success was directly attributable to Steve Jobs.

10

One More Thing

The "Let's Talk iPhone" event began, as Apple events typically do, at the stroke of 10 a.m., on Tuesday, October 4, 2011. A nervous energy ran through the crowd of about 250 guests who had squeezed into the Town Hall auditorium on Apple's Cupertino campus. There were two reasons for this: The event was the first company product debut since Tim Cook had been named CEO. Far more important, though, Apple's rabid followers fully expected a brand-new smartphone, the iPhone 5. The rumor mill had pegged the device as originally scheduled to be unveiled back in June, but in June there had been no iPhone 5, so today must be the day.

One reason for the anticipation was that the iPhone 5 allegedly possessed a new "form factor," a cause for celebration. (*Form factor* is geekspeak for the physical appearance of a device, as opposed to the composition of its innards.) A newly designed phone would represent a visible, touchable, lovable object for the cognoscenti to savor. These product unveilings are for techies what the Paris collections are for fashion editors and department store buyers—though Apple consumers needn't wait long between festive unveiling and in-store availability. What's more, Apple followers felt a sense of history: They might be bearing witness to the debut of the last product that an ailing Steve Jobs had shepherded from genesis to fruition.

Top Apple executives harbored some secrets, as they are wont to do, one of which would not be unveiled at this event: Just a few miles away, Steve Jobs lay dying at his home in Palo Alto. The company had informed the Palo Alto police a few days earlier that the Apple co-founder's death was imminent. The local authorities, Apple felt, could use the time to prepare for the inevitable outpouring of emotion from Apple fans who would transform the grounds outside his home into a shrine.

Jobs would in fact succumb the next afternoon, at about 3 p.m., to the illnesses that began eight years earlier. But on this day, with a typically brilliant blue sky over Cupertino and a giddy din inside the auditorium, the show went on. The script was written, the guests were in place, and the product demonstrations were ready. Outside the building, satellite trucks belonging to local and national news outlets parked, makeshift sound stages with klieg lights ready to beam the news to the world. Inside, journalists and other Apple guests munched on pastries and sipped coffee and juice. The journalists knew they, too, were part of a ritual; most had been to dozens of Apple product unveilings before.

When the doors opened at precisely 9:45 a.m., the photographers and camera operators were allowed in first. Then the rest of the audience was allowed to scramble for seats: Print and broadcast journalists mixed with Apple partner-guests that included Dick Costolo, the CEO of Twitter, and Ralph de la Vega, AT&T's top wireless executive. The *Wall Street Journal*'s Walt Mossberg took a seat in the middle of the auditorium, a handful of rows from the stage, on this day just another scribe invited to sing Apple's praises.

Until the music fell silent, there was nothing to distinguish this affair from the countless others Apple had produced over the years. Four songs from the 1960s and 1970s blared over loudspeakers as the crowd found their seats, took out their notebooks or laptop computers, and waved their hellos to one another. The tunes easily could have come off Steve Jobs's playlist: "Under My Thumb," by the Rolling Stones; Led Zeppelin's "Whole Lotta Love"; "Can't Explain," by the Who (which, come to think of it, could be the anthem for Apple's PR department); and "Jumpin' Jack Flash," again by the Stones. Katie Cotton, the head of public relations and also the doyenne of Apple events, sat down in her second-row seat on the aisle at 9:55 a.m. Nine of the ten seats in the front-center portion of the hall were occupied by senior Apple executives. They included software chief Scott Forstall, online services head Eddy Cue, and product marketing boss Phil Schiller. A lone absentee from the Steve Jobs brain trust was Jonathan Ive.

The first sign that this would be a different kind of Apple product unveiling was when Tim Cook strode onto the stage from behind a curtain in the wings at stage left. (His was the empty front-row seat.) Cook had anchored

Jobs-less events before—the relentless cadence of product launches continued throughout Jobs's medical leaves— but this time was different. And painful though it must have been for him, Cook acknowledged the transition. "This is my first product launch since being named CEO," he said. "I'm sure you didn't know that," he continued, to gentle laughter in the room. "I consider it a privilege of a lifetime." Cook reminded the audience that Town Hall was the site of numerous historic events in Apple's past: the launch of the iPod in 2001, a new MacBook Air in 2010. The room, he said, "is like a second home to many of us," eliciting more chuckles. "Today will remind you of the uniqueness of this company," Cook went on. "It is an extraordinary time to be at Apple."

No one in the auditorium mistook Tim Cook for Steve Jobs. But for the time being, Cook's material—alternately self-deprecatory and messianic—stood on its own. Gushing that "there is amazing momentum here" and "only Apple could do this," Cook ticked through Apple's recent accomplishments. It had opened a new store in Shanghai, which drew a hundred thousand visitors on its opening weekend. Cook showed a video of the grand opening that displayed plenty of shiny, happy Apple faces—Chinese Apple faces. "I think I've watched that a hundred times, and I think I could watch it a hundred more easily," Cook said, deploying a Jobsian conceit of subtly instructing the audience that what they had just watched was amazing— and also peeling back the curtain on Apple's methods: Cook, a literal man, likely *had* watched the clip a hundred times during endless rehearsals for the event.

Cook breezed through a review of Apple's perfor- mance, following the script and hitting Apple's key points.

"Our products are at the core of everything we do," he began. The MacBook Air, Cook continued, is "thin, light, beautiful, and wicked fast," using nearly identical language to his "off-the-cuff" observations when the laptop was unveiled a year before. Other executives, including Eddy Cue, Scott Forstall, and Phil Schiller, reviewed various product areas, including a handful of upgrades to existing products. Then Schiller addressed the news of the day. When he uttered the words "iPhone 4S," there was an awkward silence in the room as the energy seeped out of it. The phone had a faster processor, a better camera (eight megapixels...better than most $200 point-and-shoot cameras), and other new features. But it was not a new phone physically, and it wasn't an iPhone 5. Never mind that Apple typically redesigns the iPhone every two years and that the iPhone 4 was only a year old. The audience felt deflated, as if Apple had failed to meet the high expectations everyone had for the event. (Apple's share price dipped on the news—only to hit fresh highs nine trading days later.)

There was one more feature to show—which neither Schiller nor any other executive referred to as "one more thing"—and that was the Siri personal assistant feature of the new iPhone. Forstall demonstrated Siri, as he had done for Steve Jobs a few weeks before. Forstall pointedly referred to Siri as a "beta" product, one that wasn't necessarily finished but was ready for widespread customer use. That marked two subtle departures for Apple: the public release of a beta product—a favorite Google technique, the better to test and adapt to user behavior—and the adoption of a brand name of a company Apple had acquired. In the past, when Apple had acquired a company and then put its technology to work, Apple had subsumed the company and rebranded its handiwork. The mobile advertising start-up Quattro had become iAd. Streaming tunes provider Lala Music was now part of Apple's iCloud offering. SoundJam, which created digital jukebox software, long ago had given way to iTunes. But Siri, the name of the start-up Apple acquired in 2009, survived.

Letting a beta product out of the protective cocoon of Apple before it was perfect was just one of the ways that October 4 will be remembered as a defining moment in the transition from Apple's Golden Age to whatever comes next. (Apple had released beta products before, but it was not the norm.) There were other telling details: Instead of a showman on stage, there was an IBMer. Instead of all the product names being tagged with the lowercase *i* (which might as well stand for having been "inculcated" into the Apple system), another company's creation was allowed to steal the show. Was iAssistant unavailable? Would it have mattered if it were? (Siri is Norwegian for "beautiful woman who leads you to victory.")

It's tempting but inadvisable to carry this pivot-point-of-history analysis too far. Steve Jobs was heavily involved in nurturing Siri and the engineering team that created it. Moreover, Jobs had presided over similar events in the past that had been evolutionary rather than revolutionary. Also, for all its elevated importance in the new iPhone, Siri represented a continuation of a recent Apple strategy of quietly making targeted acquisitions of people and technology (as opposed to fully formed or revenue-gushing products) and integrating them into Apple offerings. More would come. In 2011, Apple made a handful of acquisitions it didn't announce. And past acquisitions had yet to see the light of day. It paid $253 million in 2010, for example, to a Canadian mapping company called Poly9, presumably to better control the mapping technology in its mobile products and services.

But there was no escaping the gaping hole Jobs left. Tim Cook's debut as CEO was workman-like but absent of whimsy. He is earnest and forceful, but the words that come out of his mouth sound scripted, because they are, rather than magical, the way they sounded when his predecessor spoke from on high. Unlike Cook, Forstall has a glimmer in his eye when he speaks. And the nerds must have taken note when Forstall mentioned his own history with artificial intelligence while praising Siri. Yet when Forstall demonstrated the "humble personal assistant," he asked it only easy questions he knew Siri could answer. Would Steve Jobs have challenged Siri by asking a question that would have elicited a dazzling but unhelpful response, just to show the whiz-bang feature's limitations? We'll never know.

Adulation was expected, but no one could have anticipated the personal nature of grief that people around the world felt when Steve Jobs died. Few of the millions who grieved for him knew him personally. He was not a movie star or statesman or athlete. Yet one million people signed an online tribute page to him on Apple's website. Mothers brought their children by his house to pay their respects—so that their children could one day tell their grandchildren of this brush with greatness. Love for Jobs was strong, and love for his company was stronger, even

among those who don't like companies. As Jobs neared
the end of his life, a grassroots protest movement with
anarchist undertones mushroomed into mass demonstrations against Wall Street specifically and capitalism generally. Right-wing critics delighted in pointing out that the
protesters used their iPhones to take pictures and their
MacBooks to create propaganda. Capitalism of the Apple
variety was okay, Goldman Sachs not so much.

The fact that a company worth $360 billion is embraced
as revolutionary and not derided as "the man" or "the
establishment" is directly attributable to Jobs and the bond
consumers felt with him. Maintaining this paradoxical relationship between Apple's market value and the perception
of its products will be a tall order for Tim Cook. Today
Apple is that rare company that enjoys an emotional connection with a wide-ranging array of consumers. As the
company takes its first baby steps away from Jobs's grave-
side, it is instructive to remember that this bond was not
always widespread. I, for one, was a longtime skeptic, and
the way that I was won over speaks volumes about how
Jobs seduced the world.

The story of Apple's resurrection resonates with me
because it coincides with my tenure in Silicon Valley. I
moved to California in the summer of 1997 to start a new
column about technology stocks in the hometown newspaper, the *San Jose Mercury News*. It was an exciting time
for the tech industry, the investing public, and most certainly for me, having arrived in California from Chicago,
where the tech scene amounted to the lumbering giant
Motorola and not much else. A bubble was just then inflat-
ing, and an entire nation was puckering up to help blow.

Online discount brokerages like E*Trade, DLJ Direct,

and Charles Schwab made investing in tech stocks a breeze. Armchair and professional investors alike were snapping up newly issued shares of fledgling companies like Netscape, Amazon.com, Yahoo!, and Excite. The most powerful info tech companies by far—Microsoft, Intel, Oracle, and Cisco—were seen as engines of the new economy. Sun Microsystems, Dell, and Compaq were surging as well. Even Hewlett-Packard, the stalwart tech shop that had provided the mythic underpinning of a "Silicon Valley" when its founders launched their start-up in a garage near the campus of Stanford University, was humming along. The Internet tailwind was filling all sails.

But not Apple's. Jobs had recently returned, and that summer my new employer went gaga over his every move. The firing of Gil Amelio was front-page news. So was the Microsoft investment. The appointment of Steve Jobs as interim CEO was celebrated the same way. I didn't get it. I certainly understood that Apple was a big local story: Its rise was the stuff of industry legend. It employed thousands of local newspaper readers, and many of the paper's subscribers were loyalists of Apple's elegant products. Apple also was the scrappy hometown team; Microsoft already was the Valley's sworn enemy, even before the browser wars with Netscape that would begin the following year. A collective cheer for underdog Apple could be heard around the newsroom—and the rest of Silicon Valley—coupled with an implied hiss for the vulgar villain from Seattle.

I brought an outsider's perspective to the hullabaloo about Apple, wondering silently if all the fuss was warranted. I hadn't used a Mac since college, eight years earlier. The computer I bought with my own money was an IBM clone (from Gateway) running Microsoft software.

When I joined *Fortune* magazine four years later, I was so stuck in my Windows ways that although *Fortune*'s editorial staff used Macs I requested a PC.

I wasn't the only one shunning Apple; the rest of the world used PCs, too. Apple was for loyalists, for artists and other creative types, as well as for educators, with whom Apple had crafted particularly close ties. The business world and average consumers who wanted to surf the Web or balance their checkbook used PCs.

Over time, however, I started to use some Apple products—just like everyone else. I downloaded iTunes onto my PC and used it to sync with my iPod, the first portable music player I'd loved since the Walkman. Then I got an iPod Touch and additional iPods (a Nano, a Mini, and even one of those tiny Shuffles that attaches to a shirt collar). Eventually I became one of those people who wanders into an Apple store for no apparent reason, admiring the elegant machines and chatting up the sales staff. Finally, I bought an iMac for my home, unwittingly acknowledging that I was the target demographic for Apple's uproarious "Mac vs. PC" ad campaign that mocked the uncool complexity of PCs compared with the hip simplicity of Macs.

The hoopla in Silicon Valley surrounding Apple's activities that summer of 1997 notwithstanding, it is shocking in hindsight just how unimportant Apple was at the time. Steve Jobs was fond of saying that when he returned to Apple, the company at one point was ninety days away from insolvency. On August 9, 2011, Apple first passed ExxonMobil as the most valuable company in the world, at $342 billion. As for Microsoft, the once-pitied Apple had passed its erstwhile foe a year earlier and quickly widened the gap in market value by more than $100 billion. In 2011, a flailing if still wildly profitable Microsoft was the tech giant that looked increasingly irrelevant.

Most companies have just one point of entry, one product to catch a customer. It is only in hindsight that I can see the subtlety with which I was converted from a PC-using apostate and the way that my conversion mirrors one of the greatest entrepreneurial runs in modern American business. Research In Motion makes smartphones. Dell makes computers. That plucky little Canadian company Kobo makes e-readers. Apple has category-killing products in each of these and several other categories. In retrospect, Apple had us at "iPod." We're all inside the AppleVerse now, meaning Apple's challenge isn't finding new customers anymore but instead figuring out what amazing new products to sell us.

The clues to understanding whether Apple can maintain its stratospheric trajectory without Steve Jobs will at first appear in its organization chart and then in the company's posture with partners and competitors. In the near term, Apple must quickly adjust to the loss of the ultimate key man. Further out, it must figure out how to adjust to the absence of its entrepreneur in chief by tweaking Apple's unusual management structure to welcome in and nourish outside entrepreneurs. That or somehow magically transforming its existing leadership into entrepreneurially minded executives. Can it evolve, in other words, from an autocracy to an incubator?

Common sense suggests that Apple simply cannot cope, in the long term, with the loss of Steve Jobs. Jobs identified himself as an entrepreneur. (His death certificate listed "entrepreneur" as his occupation.) He held a fondness for entrepreneurs because he thought they were special. He would seek them out, to meet with and give advice even to those he thought Apple would crush. They were the heroes in a world full of bozos. In that light, it's shocking that not one member of today's Apple executive team is an entrepreneur. Tim Cook is an IBMer, for gosh sakes. Scott Forstall worked for Steve Jobs his entire life. Jony Ive brilliantly served his client, and even taught him a thing or two. The wrappers may have been Ive's, but the burgers were from Steve Jobs.

So in the post-Jobs era, Apple is a massive entrepreneurial enterprise, but its people generally are not entrepreneurs—and they are not encouraged to be. The entrepreneurs Apple acquires typically don't stick around for more than a couple of years. Andy Miller of Quattro, Bill Nguyen of Lala, and Dag Kittlaus of Siri all left, despite having had rich, productive experiences at Apple, where there truly was room for only one entrepreneur. Today, instead of an entrepreneur born and bred in Silicon Valley in the executive suite, Apple has an emeritus business historian from Harvard lecturing about long-dead entrepreneurs. It is undeniably a cause for concern.

An unsung attribute of Steve Jobs that Apple also will miss is his role as a masterful networker and gatherer of information. Had times gotten really rough, Jobs would have made a fine journalist. He furiously worked the phones, calling up people he'd heard were worthy and requesting a meeting. No one turned down the chance to meet with Jobs, of course, and he used the opportunity to soak up information. His uncanny insight into trends in business and technology weren't a fluke. Jobs worked hard for his market intelligence.

Jobs played reporter until near the end of his life. On June 28, 2011, he sent word through former Adobe CEO Bruce Chizen that he wanted to speak to the young CEO of a start-up called Lytro, where Chizen was an adviser. Lytro was pioneering a consumer "light-field" camera that used sensors to automatically refocus blurry photos. It was potentially breakthrough technology and of obvious interest to Apple, whose iPhones and iPads had cameras. The company's CEO, Ren Ng, a brilliant computer scientist with a PhD from Stanford, immediately called Jobs, who picked up the phone at home and quickly said, "If you're free this afternoon maybe we could get together." Ng, who is thirty-two, hurried to Palo Alto, showed Jobs a demo of Lytro's technology, discussed cameras and product design with him, and, at Jobs's request, agreed to send him an email outlining three things he'd like Lytro to do with Apple. "What struck me the most was how clear his communication was," recalled Ng. "His eyes were just so brilliant. His glasses kind of levitated off his nose. I told him we drew a lot of inspiration from the iPad. He really smiled. It was clear it resonated."

The rest of the crew at Apple either is too busy to schmooze or was always discouraged by Jobs from doing it, lest they get too big for their britches or too distracted from their Apple work. Recall his not altogether accurate quip about "not letting Forstall out of the office." Scott Forstall does get out, but Jobs was serious about the sentiment. He circulated; Apple executives stuck to their knitting. A closed system doesn't easily absorb ideas from outside its cone of silence. Jobs supplied Apple its ideas, but he was one of a kind.

Other challenges abound, especially the fact that no matter how much Steve Jobs might have resisted the characterization, Apple is a big, complicated company now. Its marketing remains fanatically clear, clever, and effective. But Apple is in all senses of the expression a multinational company selling multiple products. The days of fitting all its products on a conference room table are behind it. Even the product tabs at the top of the Apple.com home page are instructive. They read: Store, Mac, iPod, iPhone, iPad, iTunes, Support. Clear and straightforward, yes, but these diverse categories represent far more balls in the air than Apple had a decade ago.

A diverse company calls for depth of management, and the moment Steve Jobs stepped down the weaknesses of Apple's organizational structure, which worked so well under Jobs, became apparent. Tim Cook had overseen sales for years, for example, and Apple already was searching for a sales chief. (A top Google executive, Dennis Woodside, turned down an offer to take up the position in the fall of 2011.) Jobs personally oversaw advertising for Apple. Phil Schiller has added that responsibility to his portfolio, but that will stretch him thin, and advertising—as opposed to product marketing—is not Schiller's bedrock experience. Apple has begun working out meaningful quirks. Weeks after Cook became CEO, Apple dropped the word "Mac" from Bob Mansfield's title, recognizing that his responsibilities included device engineering, too. Craig Federighi, the head of Mac software, reported to Jobs and now reports to Cook. But Scott Forstall is the king of the software hill at Apple. His role needs clarification, such as formally putting all software under him.

Jobs's death also left Apple's board without a chairman again. A month later, co–lead director Art Levinson, a former CEO himself, assumed the chairmanship. At the same time, Disney CEO Robert Iger joined the Apple board, deepening the Apple-Disney relationship.

Key Apple practices increasingly will come under pressure. When Apple slightly missed Wall Street's earnings projections in October 2011, the company attributed a falloff in iPhone 4 sales to rumors about an expected new phone. Allowing the rumor mill to affect sales is not the Apple way. Indeed, it is unheard of. What's more, fear of reprisal from Jobs was one reason employees (and ex-employees) kept their mouths shut. Tongues will become looser over time at Apple.

It will be intriguing to see how Apple will adjust its PR strategy in a post-Jobs world. Apple has more than enough money to continue to purchase and place its ads on the back cover of any magazine it likes, literally and figuratively. But the company has lost its best resource for landing Apple on the front cover. In the near future, the news media will cooperate with Apple on whatever it wants. The story is that good, with or without Jobs. But now his reality-distortion field has been deactivated, and eventually journalists will push back against Apple's stingy approach to public relations.

Partners naturally will push back, too, as they become increasingly well versed in the tactics Apple deploys against the likes of Cisco, the phone companies, and countless others. Five years from now, will a CEO devote days to rehearsing a three-minute presentation when the ultimate prize is not an audience with Steve Jobs? It seems unlikely. Ironically, Apple will confront a paradoxical image problem. In contrast to the outpouring of love for Steve Jobs after he died, the Apple family expressed outrage at the unsparing portrayal of his dark side in his authorized biography by Walter Isaacson, which was released nineteen days after Jobs's death. A similar fate could await Apple. Customers rightly love Apple for the delight its products bring them. But Apple's ubiquity increasingly will enable the many stories of its roughness, with partners and employees alike, to shift beyond the business realm and into the public psyche.

Confronting these complex issues, Apple undoubtedly will continue to defy so many of the management precepts taught in business school. However, the answer to what Apple's future will be is unlikely to come from businessthink. Instead the best answer may come from theology, for the difference between a true belief system and idolatry is that a true belief system outlasts its founder. Steve Jobs wanted Apple's values to survive him, though even his friends and admirers suspect he took some devilish pleasure in envisioning the whole thing going to pot again without him to pull the strings.

There are things Apple can do to carry on, but this would require the company that revolutionized the computer, the smartphone, and the MP3 player to be willing to revolutionize itself. Change will not come easily to one of the world's most valuable companies. If Apple's presumably incredible pipeline of products is the company's tailwind, "If it ain't broke, don't fix it" will be a headwind that could turn treacherous in the years ahead.

Its executives must learn not to ask the question "What would Steve do?" and instead just do what they think is best. In fact, Tim Cook said at an employee celebration of

Jobs's life that Jobs's parting advice to Cook was "to never ask what he would do; just do what's right." If Cook doesn't intend to be the final word on matters of taste or software architecture, then he'll have to designate who will be. Otherwise Apple will devolve into the fractious company that Steve Jobs never allowed it to be. If Apple can truly continue to behave like a start-up, then it will need to become less arrogant and bullying and more paranoid and respectful. Otherwise, it will inevitably become more like Microsoft, which too often resembles the snow leopard Jobs rejected for the packaging of Apple's software: fat and lazy.

Apple held multiple tributes for Steve Jobs in the weeks after his death. Apple.com featured the iconic Albert Watson photo of Jobs, originally shot for a 2006 spread in *Fortune*, as the sole image on its home page. His penetrating gaze stared into the camera as he gently tugged at his graying beard. Just four Apple employees attended his funeral at Alta Mesa Memorial Park in Palo Alto on October 7, 2011: Tim Cook, Jony Ive, Eddy Cue, and Katie Cotton. Pixar's Ed Catmull, Disney's Bob Iger, longtime friends Larry Brilliant and Bill Campbell, and former Intel CEO Andy Grove also attended. Jobs's family held a private event for him at Stanford University on October 16, attended by luminaries from Bono to Al Gore to Bill Clinton as well as top Apple executives and alumni. On October 19, Apple hosted an employee celebration at 1 Infinite Loop. Coldplay and Norah Jones sang—gratis. The company beamed a telecast to employees of its US retail stores.

When Tim Cook opened Apple's quarterly earnings call with investors on October 18, less than two weeks after Jobs's death, he began with a statement. "The world has lost a visionary, a creative genius and an amazing human being," Cook said. "Steve was a great leader and mentor and inspired everyone at Apple to do extraordinary things. His spirit will forever be the foundation of Apple, and we are dedicated to continuing the amazing work that he loved so much." Cook thanked everyone who offered their condolences, and then got down to the nitty-gritty business of Apple's financial results.

It was in his response to the most mundane of questions that Cook symbolically revealed what kind of steward he might be for the company Steve Jobs first created and then saved. On every financial call with Apple in recent years, investors have asked if Apple will consider returning some of its cash to shareholders, potentially in the form of a dividend. It was like a bad running joke: Investors seriously wanted a dividend, but it wasn't as if they were going to sell the stock if they didn't get one. On this call, the dividend question came right on cue, and this time, Cook had a different answer. "I'm not religious about holding cash or not holding it," he said. "I'm religious about a lot of things but not that one. And so we will continually ask ourselves what's in Apple's best interest and always do what we believe is in Apple's best interest." Cook didn't elaborate on the subjects on which he remains religious. But Apple isn't a religion. It's just a fine company with an unrivaled track record, a strong set of values, and a culture of excellence.

I wrote earlier in this chapter that common sense suggests Apple ultimately can't cope with the loss of Steve Jobs. That's true. Apple very likely will stop being an "insanely great" company. This will happen gradually, perhaps imperceptibly. A product will fail to delight. A member of the senior management team will depart, and then another. It will confront a host of problems, not the least of which will be the scrutiny of a world that obsessively watches its efforts to continue its string of success. Apple once was able to distract the public with arresting advertising and well-timed product releases, while behind the scenes it worked its magic. Now the curtain has been pulled back a little, and we see that real men and women are working furiously to keep things in motion. Customers so thoroughly anticipate new Apple offerings that despite Apple's ability to keep the details of its releases secret the anticipation puts little dents in sales anyway.

Yet forecasting Apple's fall from otherworldly status is beside the point. Apple failed plenty of times before, including during the second reign of Steve Jobs. If Apple TV was just a "hobby," as Jobs called it, then why was Apple, the great focuser of corporate energy, working on it in the first place? Did MobileMe or a faulty antenna on the iPhone 4 represent an Apple in decline? Not really. Was it a failure when Apple lost stars like Tony Fadell, Avie Tevanian, and Ron Johnson? Sure, but the business of the company continued. Companies, like people, aren't perfect. Apple in the last fourteen years of Steve Jobs's life was far better than most, but it wasn't perfect. Jobs was just particularly good at getting us to focus on the good and ignore the bad.

An Apple that is merely great, rather than insanely great, will be a disappointment, but only to the loyalists who demanded more from Apple all along. For the rest of us, our expectations of Apple were always lower. We'll keep buying merely great products for a long time.

It has been said of Apple that it is so different in the way it goes about the business of doing business that it's like a bumble bee: It shouldn't fly, but it does. Going forward, Apple will continue to fly. The explanation of how it does so, however, already is becoming just a little less mysterious.

ACKNOWLEDGMENTS

I am privileged to work at *Fortune* magazine, with some of the best, most intelligent, most dedicated, and kindest business journalists on the planet. Time Inc. editor in chief John Huey, a rabid Apple fan and a journalist who loves to tell—and hear—a good tale, blessed this book and encouraged me to write it. Andy Serwer, *Fortune*'s editor (aka my boss), dreamed up and assigned me to write the original article that grew into this book. He also graciously granted me a leave to write it. Among his many other fine attributes, Andy is an insightful editor and an inspiring and thoughtful leader. I am proud to write for a magazine he edits. Stephanie Mehta edited my original article with a cool hand and a careful eye. Like an Apple executive described in this book, she is unflappable, and I am grateful for her guidance and friendship. I wouldn't be where I am today as a journalist without the support and guidance of many other current and former *Fortune* colleagues, including, but not limited to, Rik Kirkland, Rick Tetzeli, Eric Pooley, Hank Gilman, Jim Aley, Nick Varchaver, Brian O'Keefe, Daniel Roth, Jeffrey O'Brien, Miguel Helft, Jessi Hempel, Leigh Gallagher, Jennifer Reingold, Mia Diehl, and Armin Harris.

Doris Burke is one of the finest research sleuths in the land. I couldn't have written this book—or virtually anything else I've published over the past five years—without her cheerful, meticulous, and keen assistance. Richard Nieva joined this project near its completion and quickly provided enthusiastic and critical research.

At Apple, Katie Cotton and Steve Dowling treated me cordially and consistently, and over the course of 2011 answered as many of my questions as they could. I appreciate and respect their professionalism.

A handful of books were especially helpful to me in understanding either Apple's history or the nature of Apple's leadership. These include Michael Maccoby's *Narcissistic Leaders: Who Succeeds and Who Fails*; *Return to the Little Kingdom: How Apple and Steve Jobs Changed the World* by Michael Moritz; David Price's *The Pixar Touch: The Making of a Company*; and Alan Deutschman's *The Second Coming of Steve Jobs*.

Every author should be blessed to have an agent like Esmond Harmsworth and an editor like John Brodie. Esmond first introduced himself to me after I published a cover story on Google in 2006. He wondered if I'd like to write a book about Google. I never got around to writing that book, but I was inspired by his infectious enthusiasm, and I often said that one day I'd write a book, if for no other reason than to please Esmond. His sage counsel on this project has been invaluable.

John Brodie was my colleague at *Fortune* for too few years. He single-handedly creates a witty, literate, and exuberant force field around him, making him a joy to work with. He is everything an editor should be: He cracked the whip yet lavished praise. He offered suggestions but left the decisions up to me. He encouraged and cheered me on at every turn. I am fully mindful of his immense contributions to this book, for which I am grateful. John's contributions notwithstanding, I take full responsibility for every last word that appears on these pages.

Friends and family members of authors aren't sure which is worse: the lack of attention they get from writers immersed in a book project or the dirty looks they receive in response to well-meaning queries about one's progress. I'm thankful to so many friends who nurtured, encouraged, and amused me before and during the writing of this book. These include Chuck Coustan, Jamie Dubey, Michael Newman, David Richter, Dave Kansas, Daniel Gross, Scott Thurm, Bill Campbell, Quincy Smith, Jennifer Newton, John Needham, Drew and Stephanie Hess, Pam Baker and Doug Friedman, and Oliver Fringer and Krista Donaldson.

My sisters, Paula and Amy Lashinsky, provided just the right balance of inquisitiveness, pride in their baby brother, and respect for the shortness of my time. My father, Bernard Lashinsky, has always been my most careful reader, my most ardent supporter, and my role model in life. He taught me at a young age that there is no higher compliment you can pay than to call someone a mensch. Dad, you are an über-mensch, and I love you.

This book is dedicated to three generations of females in my life. My mother, Marcia Morris Lashinsky, imbued in me her love of words, her reverence for books, and her unconditional love. She would have lusted after an iPad, and I would have cherished her feedback on this book. Instead, I cherish and honor her memory. My wife, Ruth Kirschner, is my partner and sounding board. We lovingly juggle two careers—making me even more appreciative of her understanding the time I needed to squirrel away in order to finish this book—while finding time to have a ton of fun. Lastly, because she is the newest addition to my family, is my five-year-old daughter, Leah Lashinsky, to whom I have been reading books practically since she was born. She reminds me every day what is most important in life.

AUTHOR'S NOTE

Because Apple operates differently from every other company, revealing its secrets is a tricky affair. Secrecy is a central facet of life there. Apple declined to make any of its executives or other employees available for interviews. Many former employees at Apple, from all levels of the company, as well as various people who work with Apple, did agree to speak to me for this book. None, as far as I know, received permission from the company to do so. Many spoke on the record, and their names appear here. Others agreed to help me but chose to remain unnamed. The overwhelming majority of the ex–Apple employees I interviewed professed affection for the company and a desire to see it portrayed well, knowing full well that Apple prefers that it not be portrayed at all. In an industry where everyone holds out hope of someday working with or for Apple, retribution is a legitimate concern. Strangely, at least for someone who is not as steeped in Apple-ania as I am, some ex-employees as well as current and former partners were as reluctant to be quoted speaking positively about Apple as they were to be identified criticizing Apple.

Wherever possible, I have attempted to attribute quotations or to otherwise describe in some way the characteristics or bona fides of everyone I quote. In the instances where I have quoted Steve Jobs and Tim Cook directly, without further explanation, I have first- or secondhand knowledge of their comments. Though I communicated with both Jobs and Cook during the reporting for this book, neither granted me a formal interview, either for the book or for the original article that appeared in *Fortune*.

INDEX

ABOUT THE AUTHOR

Adam Lashinsky covers Silicon Valley and Wall Street for *Fortune* magazine, where he has been on staff since 2001. Based in San Francisco, he has written cover stories for the magazine on Apple, Hewlett-Packard, and Google, as well as in-depth articles on Wells Fargo, Intel, Oracle, eBay, Twitter, and the venture-capital industry.

In addition to working as *Fortune*'s senior editor at large, he is a weekly panelist on the Fox News Channel's *Cavuto on Business* program on Saturday mornings. He also co-chairs *Fortune*'s annual technology conference, Fortune Brainstorm Tech, and is a seasoned speaker and panel moderator.

Prior to joining *Fortune*, Lashinsky was a columnist for the *San Jose Mercury News* and TheStreet.com. A native of Chicago, Lashinsky earned a degree in history and political science from the University of Illinois in 1989. He lives in San Francisco with his wife and daughter.

Inside Apple: How America's Most Admired—and Secretive—Company Really *Works* is his first book.

You can follow Lashinsky on Twitter at @adamlashinsky.

**BUSINESS
PLUS**

Recognized as one of the world's most prestigious business imprints, Business Plus specializes in publishing books that are on the cutting edge. Like you, to be successful we always strive to be ahead of the curve.

Business Plus titles encompass a wide range of books and interests—including important business management works, state-of-the-art personal financial advice, noteworthy narrative accounts, the latest in sales and marketing advice, individualized career guidance, and autobiographies of the key business leaders of our time.

Our philosophy is that business is truly global in every way, and that today's business reader is looking for books that are both entertaining and educational. To find out more about what we're publishing, please check out the Business Plus blog at:

www.bizplusbooks.com